COSTA RICA AFTER COFFEE

COSTA RICA AFTER COFFEE

THE CO-OP ERA
IN HISTORY AND MEMORY

Lowell Gudmundson

Louisiana State University Press
Baton Rouge

Published by Louisiana State University Press
lsupress.org

Spanish edition published as *Costa Rica después del café: La era cooperativa en la historia y la memoria* (2018), by Universidad Estatal a Distancia (UNED), Costa Rica.

Designer: Laura Roubique Gleason
Typeface: Minion Pro

Cover image: iStock, MattiaATH.

Library of Congress Cataloging-in-Publication Data
Names: Gudmundson, Lowell, author.
Title: Costa Rica after coffee : the co-op era in history and memory / Lowell Gudmundson
Other titles: Costa Rica después del café. English
Description: Baton Rouge : Louisiana State University Press, [2021] | "Spanish edition published as Costa Rica después del café: La era cooperativa en la historia y la memoria (2018), by Universidad Estatal a Distancia (UNED), Costa Rica." | Includes bibliographical references and index.
Identifiers: LCCN 2021010910 (print) | LCCN 2021010911 (ebook) | ISBN 978-0-8071-7625-2 (cloth) | ISBN 978-0-8071-7641-2 (paperback) | ISBN 978-0-8071-7677-1 (pdf) | ISBN 978-0-8071-7678-8 (epub)
Subjects: LCSH: Cooperation—Costa Rica. | Agriculture, Cooperative—Costa Rica. | Coffee industry—Costa Rica—History—20th century.
Classification: LCC HD3454.A4 G8313 2021 (print) | LCC HD3454.A4 (ebook) | DDC 334.097286—dc23
LC record available at https://lccn.loc.gov/2021010910
LC ebook record available at https://lccn.loc.gov/2021010911

Contents

Illustrations

Map

Figures

Graphs

Acknowledgments

My informants, whose patience and generosity were legendary, deserve thanks first. I learned many valuable lessons from them, not just historical but also personal: how not only people but objects, photographs, landscapes, and homes hold profoundly significant memories and histories; how to value the past without failing to live in the present, in order to face a future with the same optimism, humor, and energy that made that fruitful past possible. I shared many pleasant moments with them that I will never forget.

My colleagues and friends in this enterprise at the Universidad Nacional in Heredia, Wilson Picado Umaña and José Antonio Salas Víquez, deserve equal thanks. One might say, and not only in jest, that the former corrected my mistakes about Tarrazú and the latter my errors about Heredia. But we are joined by bonds deeper than geography or academics. The three of us were born and grew up in family farming zones and, owing to that accident of birth, share a whole series of almost inherited, inescapable personal questions. Carmen Kordick, another researcher of Tarrazú topics, contributed in different ways to the successful completion of this book, for which I thank her as well. The original version of this book in Spanish was stylistically improved by my friend and colleague Mauricio Meléndez Obando. In truth, however, he corrected much more than my Spanish prose contaminated by English syntax, especially with his unsurpassed knowledge of Heredia's family genealogies. Something similar must be said in thanks to Todd Manza, my copy editor with Louisiana State University Press, for turning my translation into a far more readable English.

I gratefully acknowledge the institutional support I have received to carry out this project: from the Howard Heinz Endowment of the University of Pittsburgh, the Schools of History of the Universidad Nacional and the Universidad de Costa Rica, the National Archives of Costa Rica,

ix

and the University of Oklahoma for the digitization of the 1927 and 1955 censuses in the late 1980s and early 1990s. None of this would have been possible without the firm support of then director of the archives, Luz Alba Chacón de Umaña, and her colleague Cecilia Arce. I will never forget the moment in 1986 when, after several months of transcribing probate records, they invited me for a visit to the basement of the old archive building in the center of San José to confirm the finding of the originals of the 1927 census, which led later to the discovery of the microfilm rolls of the agricultural census of 1955.

The long road to the reformulation of the project based on informant interviews would not have been possible without the fellowship provided by the National Endowment for the Humanities for academic year 2008–2009, as well as the sabbatical leaves and research funds for travel and assistants over two decades by Mount Holyoke College. I have deposited digital copies of the original images and large-scale databases from both censuses with the History Schools of the Universidad Nacional and the Universidad de Costa Rica, more than one thousand probate inventories, the recorded and transcribed informant interviews, together with images of the informants and many of their own personal documents and photographic collections. I hope future generations will be able to use this data for their own research projects.

I am grateful for the support of the staff of the Editorial de la Universidad Estatal a Distancia in Costa Rica for the initial Spanish edition of the book, in particular its then director, René Muiños Gual. I was fortunate enough to publish my first book with the newly founded EUNED in 1978. Their continued interest in this project and the professionalism they have always showed greatly aided in its initial publication in Spanish. It was always a pleasure to visit with René at the EUNED on my various visits to Costa Rica, receiving not just words of encouragement but also displays of patience and confidence in a successful outcome, a confidence that, to tell the truth, I did not always share.

This edition in English with Louisiana State University Press owes its existence to the efforts of editor Jenny Keegan. Our paths crossed once again quite serendipitously. I had previously benefited from Jenny's editorial skills when she served as an editor for the multivolume *Dictionary of Caribbean and Afro-Latin American Biography* at Harvard. Commissioning, gathering, and editing the more than one hundred biographical entries for Central America was made much easier by her guidance, and when I approached the press with the idea for an English version of *Costa Rica After Coffee,* it was a great pleasure to work with her once again. She has been the guiding force for the completion of the project and the simultaneous reissuing of *Costa Rica Before Coffee,* my first book in English. Nothing could have made me happier than to see these twin studies appear together, bookends to a nearly half-century career living in and writing about Costa Rica. Back when that first book appeared, and for some years thereafter, I was fond of saying that I had lived the "better part" of my adult life in Costa Rica, both literally and figuratively. Even today, there is a great deal of truth to the statement.

My Costa Rican family, extended and immediate, deserves not just thanks but a share of the responsibility for whatever successes there may be in the text. Over the years, conversations with my sisters-in-law, Alicia and Doris, and brothers-in-law, Jorge, Alfredo, and Harry, offered many perspectives on the experience of the 1970s and 1980s. Among so many nieces and nephews of the next generation, Gabriel, Valeria, and Max, in particular, helped me to better understand this new world they inherited and that is being transformed in their own image. Closer still, in my own household, Cecilia and our children, Paula and Darryl, have been the indispensable motivation to reflect on and write about the country of their birth and its destiny. Thankfully, our children grew up in an era when telephones were mobile but not yet intelligent, so that from an early age we developed the habit of sharing long conversations. They both knew up close the family and farm in North Dakota where I was born and grew up and, for that reason, the origin of certain of my rural obsessions and ways of seeing the world.

Among several unfinished projects of the 1980s, there was one on the comparative history of populism in the Americas. However, within the family we have recently felt another motive for completing the task of writing this text. Witnessing the most recent events in the other country they are citizens of, and the fears that these have awoken, those family conversations have strengthened my commitment to alert readers to what is at issue in our own time. Finally, I also thank the readers of this new generation who know up close, better than anyone, Costa Rica after coffee.

Introduction to the English Edition

My goal with these brief introductory comments is to provide non–Costa Rican readers with just enough background material on the nation's history and politics over the twentieth and twenty-first centuries to successfully navigate the text, its arguments, and its findings. All but chapter 3 was written in Spanish during 2016 and 2017, with some sense of urgency, as Costa Rican national politics accelerated its descent into uncertainty following the collapse of the half-century dominance of a two-party system with alternation in power. In effect, this was the same sort of radical realignments and volatility of voting blocs that is so typical of not only the United States but also many other nations in recent times. Given the reemergence of a rightist populism worldwide, readers will likely not have any great difficulty following the arguments presented in chapter 1. However, the broader context of Costa Rica's often and rightly invoked exemplary democratic development, as well as its turning points and challenges, will require some more detailed signposts for readers who may be entirely unfamiliar with the country and its history.

Over more than a century Costa Ricans have employed a whole series of arguments, images, and beliefs about themselves and their history, all to highlight both their exceptionalism in the region (and perhaps the world) and the wellsprings of their political achievements, of which there have been many. Perhaps undergirding all of them have been those two that nearly all of my published work has engaged in one way or another, both before and after *Costa Rica Before Coffee* appeared in 1986: the "White Legend" and the "rural democratic myth."

The White Legend was surely the first to emerge, likely even before the nation itself. In its crudest, most offensive form, it baldly stated and embraced white supremacist values to explain Costa Rica's relative peace and prosperity compared to its neighbors. Supposedly owing to a sparse native population in the early colonial period—and an even more imaginary lack of enslaved or free Africans—as early as the 1850s, and with increasing confidence and vehemence thereafter, the Costa Rican population was represented as overwhelmingly Spanish, Hispanic, *mestizo,* or white, depending on the proudly grateful elite author voicing the claim. While the legend was increasingly less relied upon with the post–World War II rejection of openly racist theories of national identity, it has continued to exercise a powerful hold on the minds of both Costa Rican citizens and foreign observers alike.

As that initial version of the White Legend lost respectability, if not necessarily favor, it was silently reinscribed as part of the rural democratic myth it had long been paired with in the telling of such national identity tales. In this version, Costa Rica had been very fortunate to have had so minuscule a native population, such that its early Spanish colonists were supposedly forced to work the land themselves to survive. From such inauspicious beginnings there emerged an impoverished, leveled, egalitarian society of small peasant farmers in the Central Valley, a precious historical legacy of relatively free (Spanish or *mestizo* peasant) rather than coerced (Indigenous or enslaved African) labor, and the precondition for the flowering of democratic social patterns and politics in the late nineteenth century and throughout the twentieth. Readers familiar with my earlier study will already be aware of the many different versions, rightist and leftist alike, of the rural democratic myth and how firmly these were anchored in the development of coffee-based society after the mid-nineteenth century.

Subsequent to and parallel with those foundational myths, still other myths have emerged, from an early twentieth-century one highlighting educational achievement and voting rights ("more teachers than soldiers"); to another, midcentury one claiming an inherently pacifist, nonviolent, conflict-resolving tradition ("abolition of the army" in 1949) in politics; or, most recently, several attempts, more aspirational than mythical perhaps, to invoke an environmentalist pedigree by citing the number and expanse of national parks or by invoking tourist marketing brands such as "Pure Life," "100% natural," or "carbon neutral."

Beyond the slogans and beliefs, however, since its independence in 1821 (from Spain, as part of the ill-fated Federal Republic of Central America) and its founding as a republic in 1848, Costa Rican political history has been characterized by intense conflicts as well as by those compromises and continuities so celebrated by the dominant mythical traditions. Several small-scale but bloody rivalries among the four cities of the Central Valley (San José, the national-era capital; Cartago, the colonial-era capital; Heredia; and Alajuela) marred political life from the 1820s to the 1840s. During the mid-1850s, President Juan Rafael Mora Porras led a victorious "national war" against William Walker's interventionist forces in neighboring Nicaragua, only to be deposed and subsequently executed by his domestic rivals. General Tomás Guardia Gutiérrez (1871–1882) held dictatorial power as a liberal, pursuing the construction of the railroad to the Atlantic to facilitate coffee exports, only to witness the creation of the banana export behemoth, the United Fruit Company, alongside the railroad tracks through the Atlantic lowlands.

While two-time president Oscar Arias Sánchez (1986–1990 and 2006–2010) officially proclaimed 1989 to be the centennial of Costa Rican democracy, the consolidation of competitive elections and the relatively peaceful transfer of power by incumbents was far from secure after 1889. The date in question corresponds more accurately to the consolidation of a relatively firm elite consensus around the same liberal principles of governance that had guided much of the Guardia dictatorship's policies as well. At least as important as elite consensus in democratic consolidation were steps taken in the early twentieth century toward nearly universal male suffrage and the secret ballot, along with dramatic mass literacy advances. This focus on public primary education after the 1880s was a central policy goal of these self-described liberal leaders, culminating in a several decades-long dominance of presidential elections by a so-called Olympic group of enlightened founding fathers, most visibly three-time president Ricardo Jiménez Oreamuno (1910–1914; 1924–1928; and 1932–1936).

The severe dislocations of World War I led to the last military coup and the dictatorial regime of the Tinoco brothers in 1917–1919. After deposing the civilian regime of Alfredo González Flores (1914–1917), Federico Tinoco Granados, the naval minister who led the coup and the de facto regime, was himself overthrown by a broad-based urban insurgency that culminated in riots and the assassination of his brother, War Minister José Joaquín Tinoco Granados, and Federico's flight into exile in France three days later. The successful insurgency would have important implications for politics for decades to come, particularly during the Depression of the 1930s.

While key leaders of the violent urban uprising against the Tinoco dictatorship came from students and staff of the Girls' High School (Colegio de Señoritas) in San José, women's suffrage was not achieved until 1949, as part of the constitutional reform following the civil war of 1948, with women voting nationwide for the first time in 1953. However, a key female insurgent leader, children's literature author and educator Carmen Lyra (María Isabel Carvajal), would be a cofounder of the Costa Rican Communist Party in 1932. The novelty of the party's electoral participation being tolerated, along with the survival of regular elections and civilian rule in Costa Rica, unlike in all the other Central American republics of the time, can hardly be overstated. Similarly, the Depression led the state to create institutions to regulate processor/producer relations and prices in the dominant coffee export sector, a key antecedent of the spectacularly successful producer co-op movement of the 1960s that is so central to this study.

The decade of the 1940s and its culmination with the civil war of 1948 set the course for the trajectories of the two dominant political coalitions during the remainder of the twentieth century. Chapter 1 describes in considerable detail the triumphant National Liberation Party (Partido Liberación Nacional, or PLN), led and defined by three-time president José Figueres Ferrer (1948–1949; 1953–1958; and 1970–1974), and the defeated and exiled regime led by Rafael Angel Calderón Guardia, who was president from 1940 to 1944 and was a candidate once again in the disputed election of 1948. *Liberacionistas* versus *calderonistas* defined electoral politics for a half century or more, not least because each of the strongmen's sons would eventually claim party leadership and win the presidency in their own right (Rafael Angel Calderón Fournier in 1990–1994 and José María Figueres Olsen in 1994–1998). The Social Christian Unity Party (Partido Unidad Social Cristiana, or PUSC) was formed in the late 1970s and early 1980s and backed Calderón Fournier's successful presidential bid in 1990, bringing together his own largely urban, popular loyalists, major coffee and investor groups opposed to the PLN's state interventionist policies, and fairly often that same Communist Party, based solidly in the banana workers' union, that had most effectively mounted an armed defense of Calderón Guardia's failed bid for reelection in the 1948 conflict. Both the PLN and the PUSC would splinter, decline, and fail to win or even credibly contest presidential elections after 2010. However, before describing their fall from grace, we'll look at the earlier collapse of the local communist party (Vanguardia Popular) at the dawn of the neoliberal era, which offers a cautionary tale about what its twilight would bring for the two major parties as well. The rift within the left emerged after their considerable success, both politically and economically, during the 1970s. Longtime Vanguardia leader Manuel Mora Valverde was a cofounder of the Communist Party in 1932 and had repeatedly pursued policies relatively independent of Moscow, during and after the 1940s alliance with Calderón Guardia and reformist elements in the Catholic Church. The bitter dispute provoked by Mora Valverde's support of President Luis Alberto Monge Alvarez's (1982–1986) declaration of permanent neutrality in 1983, to fend off the Reagan administration's demands for more direct support for its Contra war efforts in Nicaragua, marked the beginning of the schism. However, no long-standing insurgencies within the party, pushing for a more direct role in support of Central American revolutionary struggles in neighboring Nicaragua or El Salvador, played much of a role in its subsequent demise.

Far more important were domestic events that radically undermined both the party's influence and the banana workers' union itself. The financial default and utter collapse of the local economy in 1980–1982 led to an ever-increasing reliance on direct U.S. financial aid from the Reagan administration under both PUSC and PLN presidencies throughout the 1980s, with a corresponding series of structural adjustment agreements signed with the International Monetary Fund and World Bank. White-collar, public-sector labor unions had traditionally been dominated by the PLN rather than by the Left, and when the United Fruit Company announced its withdrawal from all banana production on the Pacific coast in 1984, the handwriting was clearly on the wall for the party. With ever more fuel for the fire, mutual recriminations and internecine leadership struggles accelerated, leading to the nearly complete disappearance, for several decades, of any organized Left party in Congress or in national life. Banana production on the Atlantic coast was already largely in domestic capitalists' hands, and just as with the turn-of-the-century pineapple export boom, union organization was effectively suppressed, employing the age-old strategy of recruiting noncitizen laboring populations, pioneered in the nineteenth century with West Indians, followed by Nicaraguans after World War I, and overwhelmingly with Nicaraguans from the late 1980s to the present, now not just for agricultural employment but for all manner of construction and manual labor occupations nationwide.

The neoliberal era may have offered an early reprieve to the PLN and PUSC, but their day on the docket would come just as surely. For two decades or more, they continued to contest presidential elections and alternate in power, with consecutive PUSC presidents from 1998 to 2006, followed by consecutive PLN presidents from 2006 to 2014. Neoliberal, business-friendly politics as usual eventually became an Achilles' heel for the traditional major party presidents, culminating in bribery and influence-peddling charges being filed against three ex-presidents in 2004. The two PUSC ex-presidents accused, Calderón Fournier and Miguel Angel Rodríguez Echeverría (1998–2002), returned to Costa Rica to face the charges and were either able to avoid conviction on appeal or, if convicted, at least lengthy jail time. The PLN ex-president, Figueres Olsen, chose to avoid prosecution entirely by continuing to live and work in Europe until the statute of limitations ran out and political infighting had subsided at home, thanks at least in part to his high-level international connections and Spanish dual citizenship.

The televised spectacle of ex-presidents being detained and whisked away to jailhouse bookings, or evading prosecution by refusing to return to the country or to be extradited, no doubt contributed mightily to the two parties' fall from grace. However, a whole series of questionable privatizations, commissions cum payoffs, and banking reform scandals had preceded the graft and bribery cases themselves, tarnishing the image of both parties and ensuring that neither Calderón nor Figueres would be able to marshal support or control events within their parties following their time in office.

By the late 1990s, both parties were already bleeding support to center-right or center-left alternatives, the PLN most dramatically at first, but the PUSC even more disastrously thereafter. Much of the left-liberal wing of the PLN abandoned the party to form the Citizens' Action Party (Partido

Acción Ciudadana, or PAC) in advance of the 2002 elections. While it was never successful in gaining anything near a congressional majority, or even the largest caucus, to nearly everyone's surprise the PAC managed to elect consecutive presidents in 2014 and 2018, despite both candidates being virtual unknowns in national politics to that point.

The PLN has maintained the largest number of deputies in Congress, although no group has had the power to govern with anything like the coherence reminiscent of the earlier two-party system. The PUSC has suffered a more severe if slower demise, without such a highly visible en masse defection from its ranks. Vast numbers of its traditional popular voters have flocked to a proliferation of personalist and evangelical political parties, not only in the Central Valley cities but also in the coastal areas, which are seeing rapid employment growth thanks to new fruit exports and international tourism. PUSC presidential primary and general election deputy candidates have become increasingly invisible or irrelevant in recent years. Thus, Costa Rica is living its own radical realignment of political forces and the waning or disappearance of traditional electoral loyalties, so typical of the postneoliberal era worldwide. Exploring the logic and origins of that reconfiguration is a central goal of what follows.

Beyond the outline of Costa Rican politics and history offered here, English-language readers surely deserve an early alert regarding the materials presented in chapter 5. Costa Rican readers might well have thought such an alert redundant, as they have lived through the radical and rapid social changes described there. For those readers, my task was only to gently jar their sense of the everyday, naturalized social order that the younger among them no doubt have internalized and rarely, if ever, question. Rather than seeking only to show them how rapid and pervasive those changes have been, the larger goal was to reveal where the changes came from historically.

For readers of this work, however, an awareness of just how comparable postmodern Costa Rican society might well seem to a postindustrial and postmodern reader in the United States or elsewhere can not safely be left to the last chapter, presuming a lived experience and familiarity that clearly does not exist. I would hesitate to invoke the postmodern adage or recipe of reading the chapters of a book in any order—better yet, last to first. However, suffice it to say that in the space of three or four decades,

Costa Rica has experienced a demographic transition and development process that has made it equal or superior to most North Atlantic societies, the United States in particular, in life expectancy, aging of the population, postponement of marriage and increase in common-law or informal unions, fewer pregnancies and reduced family sizes, educational attainment in general and female education in particular, and female labor market participation. Furthermore, it has witnessed a radical reduction of agriculture as a share of gross domestic product and employment and dramatic increases in income and regional inequalities. It has done all of this while becoming a key supplier to North Atlantic markets of not just gourmet-quality coffee or bulk shipments of bananas and pineapple but also of high-tech medical devices and medical tourism, building from scratch a massive, environmentally marketed tourism industry, and becoming entrapped in a vast drug transshipment network, all tightly integrated with and dependent on those same North Atlantic partners.

Recognizing in the nonindustrial tropics a fully formed postmodernity in its own right may test our comprehension, not to mention our pride of place in the North. However, rest assured that unless we recognize and come to grips with such an equally jarring moment of our own, readers will not be able to fully grasp the breadth of social changes set in motion by the co-ops and their modernization of Costa Rica's then dominant coffee sector. That same process led directly to rapid urbanization and the relative depopulation of the traditional countryside, to a "Costa Rica after coffee" in all the obvious and in other, not so apparent, meanings of our title.

Another, even more jarring, moment of reflection and self-recognition was provided by the coronavirus pandemic of 2020. On the one hand, Costa Rica's centuries-old investments and achievements in education and health care have demonstrated their worth time and again, leading to remarkably low mortality levels compared not only to its neighbors or to Latin America in general but also to nations worldwide. However, the déjà vu or tragedies resulting from COVID-19 are painfully apparent as well. All of the proud economic successes of the neoliberal era—from international tourism, agricultural exports, and construction reliant on guest or undocumented workers to spiraling growth of the informal sector amid rapid urbanization, and its consequent regional and income inequalities—became vectors not so much of virus contagion itself but of the sudden economic collapse that accompanied it, on a scale that is hard to comprehend.

The complete closing of borders and air travel for many months, along with the impossibility of maintaining lockdowns and effective quarantines in a society already fiscally vulnerable and newly dependent on informal sector employment and guest workers, with their precarious housing and need to travel from farm to farm and harvest to harvest, made for a situation that not even Costa Rica's enviable institutional capacity could easily manage. In the blink of an eye, the international tourism industry, previously the darling of a certain type of environmentalist promoter and investor, became the source of deep fears about short-term recovery scenarios and the newly visible vulnerability of its future growth and employment. (This is not unlike the concerns long expressed over drug trafficking and its nefarious impacts on Costa Rican society, both high and low.) Likewise, the extremely rapid aging of the native-born Costa Rican population made even more visible not only the successes of its health care system in the midst of the pandemic but also the severe challenges society as a whole will face in attempting to stimulate local production and employment. Because so much of the population is retired or not participating in the labor market at all, and because most of those working in services and high-tech sectors have high levels of formal education but little or no work experience in industrial or agricultural settings, even when the current crisis eases there will be daunting challenges in adjusting to whatever the "new normal" of the international economy brings. The disruptive costs of any strategy for decoupling, reverse globalization, or "localization" of production will necessarily be greatest for those nations that have been most successful in reaping the rewards of neoliberal globalization in the recent past, Costa Rica foremost among them.

In effect, chapter 5, with its "Transformations and Unexpected Consequences" subtitle, invites one reading, whether as an X-ray of the twentieth century or an MRI of the twenty-first, revealing in detail the co-op era and its legacies. It also invites the reader to reflect on just how doggedly societies are capable of discounting or looking away from deep structural imbalances and inequalities, vulnerabilities that are safely ignored until their unsustainability is made painfully visible by catastrophic events of one kind or another. My expectation in writing this book was certainly not to witness such events almost immediately myself. However, that too seems a fitting parallel, since my earlier work *Costa Rica Before Coffee* was written in 1980 and 1981, while I was living in Costa Rica, during a similarly wrenching crisis at the birth of the neoliberal era. Perhaps I, along with a new generation of readers, am gaining a newfound appreciation of the apocryphal saying "May you live in interesting times."

COSTA RICA AFTER COFFEE

1

Green Revolution as Antidote to Red in the Green and White Era of National Liberation

Costa Rica's Coffee Co-ops and Anticommunist Reform

For some, the title of this book, *Costa Rica After Coffee,* might suggest an apocalyptic, dystopic vision of a Costa Rica without coffee, denuded, without resources, ruined, historically unrecognizable. But the title intends a different point. On the one hand, it contains a certain allusion or autobiographical dichotomy, since many years ago my first monograph was titled *Costa Rica Before Coffee.*[1] It no longer represents a starting point but rather an arrival, in terms of research themes and periods and of many life experiences in a professional career of nearly a half century dedicated to Costa Rican history. On the other hand, "after coffee" refers not to coffee's disappearance, nor to any historical failure, but rather to its singular success in transforming a country toward a present, our own, and a future that is radically less agricultural and rural—to which one might add less youthful, less poor, less Central Valley–dominated, less exceptional, and other things. In effect, what I attempt here is an analysis of the process by which the coffee sector and its social actors, especially co-op members, set in motion deeply transformative socioeconomic and political changes in the second half of the past century, the consequences of which, intended or not, have altered the country so drastically in the past few decades.

Among those changes is the apparent swing by the National Liberation Party (PLN), beginning in the 1980s and 1990s, from a self-proclaimed social democratic tradition toward its current center-right position, ever more rightist. I call this the green and white era because green and white are the party's colors. The historiographic critique begun by Jacobo Schifter, among others, was very explicit in *Costa Rica Before Coffee* and echoed the reinterpretation of the origins and ideology of the PLN that was in vogue at the time.[2] In effect, the data gathering for this project

began precisely in the second half of the 1980s and led to several different publications over the years.[3] In all of these pieces, I sought to offer a
fuller and deeper portrait of the history of small and medium-size coffee growers, mythical heroes of both the briefly hegemonic *liberacionista* ideology and that of the much older view of Costa Rican democratic
exceptionalism.

As often happens with overly ambitious projects that begin in one historical era and end in another, *Costa Rica After Coffee* has had its share of
dead ends and reformulations along the way. Though it began as fashion-
able quantification in the service of so-called social and economic history
and the ideological critiques that were typical as the Cold War waned,
prior to the linguistic and postmodern turns, it ended up with a return
to oral and testimonial history that had been my first steps into Costa
Rican history.[4]

This project and analysis carries a certain risk of anachronism for readers, given the passage of time, so we will need to better frame its objectives
and assumptions in the context of the current situation and not the context present at its birth. I hope to offer the reader a detailed social, economic, and statistical portrait of those figures as foundational as they are
elusive in Costa Rican historiography—the small and medium-size coffee farmers of the Central Valley—but also an interpretation of the PLN's
ideological origins and trajectory, which carry a different hue today. After
a brief parallel analysis of the imprecision of the labels used both then and
now, I offer other historical perspectives on the logic inherent in the often
commented upon and readily evident conversion of *liberacionismo,* from
a center-left social democratic party to one on the center-right, and the
role coffee growers and their cooperatives have played in this.

Populism, Reformism, Rightist, Leftist: Politics and Antipolitics

In recent times, many people have ceased speaking and writing of a postmodern social context, referring instead, in ominous tones, to a context
of "post-truth." This refers to the rise of a very aggressive form of so-called
rightist populism, which is nationalist, nostalgic, and nearly always xenophobic; antiglobalization and protectionist; openly misogynist and racist
in some cases, and in extreme cases even antiscientific or antirational-

ist, in the style of the famous Spanish Franquist slogan "Long live death." Curiously, this phenomenon gained strength in the North Atlantic just as Latin America's center-right ideologues stopped using the term "populist" tendentiously and dogmatically as an epithet, or simply as synonymous with misrule, to refer to center-left regimes not to their liking that were elected in the late 1990s in places such as Argentina, Bolivia, Ecuador, Nicaragua, and Venezuela.

Even more suspiciously, these same commentators and opinion makers were incapable of recognizing, much less publicly admitting, the enormous similarities between the two phenomena. In both cases, their electoral base tended to feed on those harmed (or those only threatened or angered culturally, not necessarily directly or materially) by the impacts of free trade, structural adjustment, globalization, and cultural secularization of recent decades, especially among the fastest-growing electoral group: infrequent voters without party identification ("independents" to some, poorly informed and naive to others, volatile in any case), as well as less educated males and those with more precarious ties to the formal economy.

The coalitions that several times elected both the brand-new Latin American leftists from the late 1990s and the ultraconservative U.S. Republicans, from George W. Bush to Donald J. Trump, reveal more sociological similarities than differences, independent of the labels and supposed ideologies. And there is nothing strange about it, given that they are generated by the same global transformation, whether we call it neoliberalism, free markets, savage capitalism, deregulation, or globalization. Just as with those mythical elephant cemeteries, there is a certain poetic justice in the fact that the last and most violent reaction to neoliberal displacements should have taken place precisely in its sites of origin and imperial policies.

No nondogmatic observer can fail to see the extraordinary cynicism and short-term view of rightist politicians in the Christian West, in their self-congratulatory use of new, tendentious labels in place of the tired old ones of the Cold War. They have tirelessly denounced Islamic fundamentalism and a supposed war of civilizations while simultaneously hunting for votes among and denying the existence of their own forms of vengeful fundamentalism, whether evangelical or xenophobic.[5]

While the political forces of both extremes sought to reposition themselves in the new post–Cold War situation, other profound processes of social and political change were being born within postmodern societies. They were more well known in North Atlantic societies that suffered rapid processes of deindustrialization, but postmodernity everywhere was associated with rapid urbanization and notable advances in educational levels and female labor market participation, tending toward a secularization and alteration of traditional cultural norms. New social groups and experiences appeared everywhere, but without a working daily life, without shared physical spaces as before, and with no political organization to bring them together. They shared ideas, preferences, experiences, perhaps even self-affirmed identities, but without the common causes or means to make themselves felt directly or continuously in traditional politics, which no few viewed with disdain.

There was a redefinition of participation, consciousness, and militancy with regard to questions of identity (ethnicity, gender, and sexuality, the holy trinity of the liberal agenda of the 1990s), first visible in leftist or liberal university and intellectual circles. Identity was no longer economic, much less union-based, and was in line with all those changes experienced at work, home, and culturally, all tending toward self-segregation by income and toward cultural self-segmentation within a consumer society that was contradictorily collectivist and individualist, interactive but at the same time isolated. Whether expressed as virtual realities or reality shows, the end-of-century tone was far from that of the world that had formed previous generations and is perhaps best summarized in the title of a recent book on family life in the era of smartphones, *Alone Together*.[6]

Parallel identity processes rapidly appeared on the right, around religiosity, nationalism, immigration, and ethnicity, as well as so-called traditional values under attack or clearly discredited, with the additional factor of protest over the loss of employment owing to deindustrialization. Needless to say, all that was lacking was a leader, populist or not, who would unite the traditional bourgeois right with newly "indignant" followers to turn the situation around. Compared to the self-isolated leftism of the cultural elites, the renovated right with a popular base would be likely to win many electoral contests.

Lamentable and painful examples of analytical confusion are plentiful in our postmodern and dangerously post-truth era. Thus, we need to attempt to clarify some of the possible historical meanings of the terms

4

"populism" and "reformism" to better orient the reader on the topic of recent Costa Rican history. In both world and Latin American history, the term "populist" has had almost as many meanings as concrete cases. Without exception, the term refers to popular movements that defend the interests of the people, the majorities, always against the status quo and its dominant elites—in other words, the angry and indignant, potentially as likely on the right as on the left in terms of ideology. Once in power, such movements reveal their Janus-faced nature, that is, their opposed tendencies toward both extremes of the ideological panorama. With a few examples, ranging from curious to pathetic on both sides, we can better comprehend such tendencies and contradictions.

The first U.S. case is William Jennings Bryan, the three-time losing presidential candidate of the Democratic Party (in 1896, 1900, and 1908) who was the unquestionable leader of the Populist movement. No matter how he presented himself as the defender of the people and the common man, however, his ideas about social change and modernity were anything but modern. He played an important role in support of the passage of Prohibition (1920–1933) with the Eighteenth Amendment to the Constitution, avoided his party publicly condemning the Ku Klux Klan for fear of losing Southern support, and just before his death in 1925, had an important role in the infamous Scopes Monkey Trial, defending the prohibition of the teaching of Darwin's theory of human evolution in the state of Tennessee.[7]

The U.S. Department of State offered another spectacle of incomprehension, somewhere between pathetic and laughable, in denouncing the populist governments of Juan Domingo Perón in Argentina and Getulio Vargas in Brazil—first as pro-fascist before World War II and then as pro-communist during the Cold War. The reason was simple. Populism shares a characteristic commonly associated with paper: it absorbs any color of ink. In this case, Vargas's decision to support the U.S. invasion of Italy with military resources resolved the problem of pro-fascist accusations long before Perón, since from the start U.S. geostrategic needs were the source of such a voluntary, self-interested confusion of labels.

In the classic cases of the United States and Russia, the populist concept or label refers above all to rural protest movements in the second half of the nineteenth century and the early twentieth. They arose in response to depressed agricultural prices and the rapid transformation of the social and technological structure of agriculture, as well as the processes of urbanization and industrialization that threatened as never before the cultural and political hegemony of rural areas and tradition. Transferred to the field of Latin American history, the classic cases tended to be urban and tied to labor and entrepreneurial groups emergent with the industrialization process, accelerated by the demand crisis after 1930, and the import substitution process maintained during the following three decades or more.[8] Once again, the governments of Perón in Argentina and Vargas in Brazil would be archetypes, but we find echoes of the same process in many other Latin American countries.

If this change of protagonists were not sufficient motive for confusion, Latin American experience offers other complications, with particular relevance for the Costa Rican case. The cases of Mexico during the rule of Lázaro Cárdenas (1934–1940) and his reanimated land reform, the Movimiento Nacional Revolucionario after it took power in Bolivia in 1952, and Castro's Cuba during the 1960s offer somewhat atypical examples. Once in power, these populist movements headed revolutionary processes combining in novel form urban or nonagricultural union movements with profound land reforms and nationalist expropriations (oil in Mexico; tin in Bolivia; and sugar, oil, and mining in Cuba).

However, within an even broader typology, there are cases, such as Costa Rica in the 1940s and 1950s, where a rural and agricultural base of support appears and is consolidated as a critical source for populist movements and their preferred governments. Like Costa Rica, Puerto Rico and Colombia witnessed political contests and regimes in which different forces and leaders attempted to organize critical rural and agricultural populations as the support base for national redemption. In Puerto Rico, this occurred under the rule of Muñoz Marín after 1940, and in Colombia it appeared with liberals like Alfonso López Pumarejo (1934–1938) and later the charismatic and incendiary left-liberal Jorge Eliécer Gaitán. Whether these movements are called reform or revolution depends on the case.

Two factors are combined in precise ways in the cases of Costa Rica, Puerto Rico, and Colombia: coffee is identified with "the nation" and the peasantry, whereas bananas or sugar are identified with the "foreign" and the corporate. The corporations are U.S. in all cases, as with oil in Venezuela, but oil in Mexico or copper and nitrates in Chile involved important participation by European investors as well. In all these cases we have called "nonclassic" (Bolivia, Colombia, Costa Rica, Cuba, and Mexico, and Puerto Rico as a case apart, for the obvious reason that it was never an independent nation), where foreign-owned property predominated in one of the major, large-scale export industries, the possibilities for both broad nationalist reform and competitive political radicalization increased substantially.[9]

The unfinished political project of Gaitán—the assassinated left-liberal—proposed an alliance between peasant beneficiaries of his party's land reform during the López Pumarejo government and the banana workers of coastal Colombia. It is no secret that very similar groups made up the most solid social bases for the political combatants of the civil war of 1948 in Costa Rica. Classic populism of the World War II era emerged with President Calderón in the 1940s, with the firm support of the banana workers' union. His triumphant opponents in 1948, those who would later form the PLN under the leadership of José Figueres, cultivated an anticommunist right populism that relied on the support of coffee farmers and the areas where they predominated.

There is no doubt that both groups in conflict in 1948 claimed for themselves the mantle of "reform" or "reformist," with neither accepting the label of "reactionary" or of "restorationist" of the old regime. Beyond the central topic of the moment—the freedom and fairness of the election—both presented themselves as democratic and popular, but only *calderonismo* has been described as "populist." Both reformist, yes, but both populist?

Before attempting a response, we must distinguish a bit better between politics and antipolitics, between mythic message as motivation and self-conviction, on the one hand, and public policies in search of stable future support, on the other. The former is a fundamental characteristic of populism in all times and places; the latter is actually the cardinal distinction of reformism, so competitive and fruitful in the Costa Rican case.

The Politics of Antipolitics: Populism in Rebellion

The most perceptive analyses of the current populist wave in Latin America undoubtedly emphasize its protest component. While inequality is a necessary condition for its appearance, it is anything but sufficient to motivate those who suffer from it to participate in the electoral arena.

Only with leaders willing to denounce inequality and promise solutions—which are most often somewhere between vague and magical—does it express itself in large numbers of voters who would otherwise stay at home. Frustrations alone are not sufficient motivation; it requires a strategic decision on the part of political leaders to give a name to the problem and to its supposed causes and solutions, such that infrequent voters will participate and vote for them.[10]

The most accurate analyst of the current populist wave in the Costa Rican context is the political scientist Constantino Urcuyo.[11] A public intellectual as well as an academic, Urcuyo emphasizes the messages and methods typical of populism, whether rightist or leftist, when they intend to remove those who hold political power—undeservedly, from their perspective. They always propose a Manichean vision of good versus evil, comprising a homogenous, morally superior people and those elite minorities who share neither that elevated moral status nor the material interests of the great majorities, the people, and so forth. This homogenous vision of the mythical people employs, and at the same time rejects, the idea of social stratification or Marxian class struggle in favor of a series of highly varied villains of the movie. These range from the political or economic elite (the "top of the pyramid"—oligarchs, aristocrats, the dynasty, the rulers, dictators, the rich, monopolists, or in the classic *liberacionista* slang, the "*calderocomunistas*") to different ethnic groups, immigrants, intellectuals, homosexuals, the press, the cultural industry, and the like. All are ideal candidates to play the role of traitors, fifth-columnists, or enemies of the people.

This facet of populism takes advantage of visceral and primitive instincts embellished with traditionalist, antimodernist demands with deep roots, which existed long before the creation of nation-states. It expresses not only political polarization or a particular historical moment but also a very generalized unease in the midst of social transformations much more profound than a mere party confrontation, no matter how violent. Its current manifestations retain similarities—inevitably, though luckily distant, so far—with medieval witch hunts and burnings and the Inquisition's autos-da-fé. These are social cleansings carried out by the Inquisitors' modern equivalents, who wage dirty wars or assassinate indigents and gang members alike whose existence bothers them. It is a consummate irony that authorities being investigated for corruption or other improper acts, including populist politicians, often defend themselves by claiming to be victims of false accusations, of a "witch hunt," when they are precisely those who have appealed most to these same atavistic instincts to gain power.

This form of populism employs not only a Manichean moralism but also a paranoid style in which traditional culture and its norms are under attack by innumerable conspiracies and hidden, malicious forces, whether this is called the "deep state," spies, or criminal organizations. The existing, discredited elites are not simply self-serving, inept, isolated, or worn out, but squalid, demonic, immoral, illegitimate, or corrupt—in other words, morally indefensible and removable by force as quickly as possible.[12] Joseph McCarthy's style of anticommunism in the 1950s United States, and Costa Rica's variety during the same era, were built on racism, misogyny, and all manner of absolutisms that always find enemies, real or imagined, even if one needs to search for them under the bed.

Today, the principle concern of Urcuyo and other Costa Rican political scientists has been to better understand the possibilities of a "Trump effect" in the presidential election of 2018. With the disintegration of the traditional bipartisanship of the PLN and the Social Christian Unity Party (PUSC) following corruption trials of PUSC ex-presidents and the collapse of the *liberacionista* presidential campaign in 2014 against the virtually unknown winning candidate of the Citizen Action Party (PAC), electoral volatility is not a hypothetical question but a crude, undeniable reality. Urcuyo, in particular, points out that undecided and politically indifferent voters are easy prey for demagogues of the most varied stripes, who feed all manner of resentments, obsessions, and dissatisfactions without any program to resolve them but with clear intentions to gain power by adding wood to the fire.

However great our interest in the current local phenomenon, in a more general sense it is surprising how quickly today's societies have forgotten the 1930s experience with rightist populism and its disastrous legacies. At the height of the most recent third world leftist revolutions, in the 1970s and 1980s (in particular, the Sandinista revolution), authors as lucid as Ernesto Laclau tended to overestimate the possible benefits of the union of "national" and "popular" causes under leftist flags.[13] In our own era, rereading the observations of Antonio Gramsci or Walter Benjamin is far more instructive, since these works were written by authors who fled from rightist populisms that ended up in different catastrophic European fascisms.

Populism in rebellion simplifies, demonizes, and appeals to emotions in support of singular and violent solutions. Given the self-complacent image of eternal national pacifism expressed in slogans such as "More teachers than soldiers" and "Without an army," it may be difficult for many in Costa Rica today to imagine a representation of its political history in crudely populist terms. However, it is much less difficult to find evidence, images, and discursive language typical of it before and after 1948. David Díaz offers us innumerable examples of the polarization and hatred codified in the declarations of the eventual victors, from the regrettable order given in 1947 by Otilio Ulate, who was editor of the newspaper *El Diario de Costa Rica,* opposition presidential candidate in 1948, and, years later, president ("If s/he is a *calderocomunista,* do not speak to, buy from, or sell to him/her"), to the dehumanization of the vanquished, the *mariachis,* by the *liberacionista* newspaper *La República* in 1951.

All manner of denigrating, xenophobic, and racist epithets (such as "Black" or "Nicaraguan" intended pejoratively, along with terms such as "communist dockworkers," "shirtless," "shoeless," and "rabble") were employed by the opposition newspaper headed by Ulate, while those Díaz describes as "hard-liners" carried out terrorist and armed actions with the intention of provoking a civil war that would give them, unlike the official candidate Ulate, what they could not gain at the ballot box: political power without constitutional limits or legitimate, organized opposition. After their victory, in a tone mixing moral superiority with Darwinian positivism, the victors in charge of *La República* celebrated the supposedly inevitable disappearance of their opponents by saying that "the *mariachi* is a typical example of the misfit. His moral makeup does not allow him to live in the environment of the new Costa Rica. To his misfortune, for the good of the nation, the *mariachi* species is definitively destined to disappear from the Costa Rican political fauna."[14]

That we have learned to forget or ignore such evidence over the past few decades says much more about certain achievements of the era of green and white hegemony than about earlier history and its reinterpretation. This intellectual hegemony tends to limit our repertoire, but examples abound even within the very folklore of heroic *liberacionismo.* I refer not only to the systematic delegitimization of the earlier president

Dr. Calderón Guardia (employing the moniker of "*calderocomunistas,*" or accusations of corruption or electoral fraud, or his repeated "invasions") or of Archbishop Sanabria (ally of the "atheistic" communists) but also to the very figure of the PLN's ultimate leader, José Figueres Ferrer, clearly identified at the time with the hard-liners. More than enough references have been made to his undeniable contributions to the construction of a vibrant and exemplary democracy, always emphasizing his abolition of the army, sledgehammer in hand to demolish the old outpost in San José, the Cuartel Bellavista. But his most lucid and enthusiastic biographer, Charles Ameringer, captured the logic of his rightist populism in rebellion when he described a 1946 meeting of opposition leaders to discuss electoral strategies for the new Social Democratic Party. After listening to several far too lengthy and complicated positions and proposals, Figueres took out his revolver and slammed it down on the table in front of him, saying, "Boys, you are wrong; this is the only way."[15]

Populism in Power: Competitive Reformism and Transformative Policies

Although *liberacionistas* and *calderonistas* could both fit within a broad definition of populism, their routes to power and their reform policies were were substantially different. In both cases, they sought to create a solid bloc of favorable voters and a transformation of the social and economic bases of the nation in order to favor themselves. In that sense, and independent of their route to power, their most important legacies were as reformists and not as populists.

Calderonismo shared many aspects of the trajectory of classic figures such as Perón in Argentina, Vargas in Brazil, or Cárdenas in Mexico. Neither magicians nor ventriloquists, they reached power through the existing regime; in effect, they themselves could be found among the elites that populism ought to oust, and even so, they proceeded to weave alliances with new social groups previously excluded from state power. It was as if the very same *indignados* (indignant citizens) occupied the presidential chair without having marched in protest or fired a single shot. But in the Costa Rican case, *calderonismo* was not the first or only case in which this route to reform was attempted. A long tradition of reformism "from the heights of power" already existed, in the dictatorship of Tomás Guardia

(1871–1885), during the so-called "Olympic" administrations of the early twentieth century, and never more clearly than with the administration of Alfredo González Flores (1914–1917), who was overthrown at the end of World War I.

The Figueres administrations (1948–1949, 1953–1958, and 1970–1974) and *liberacionismo* after 1948 also shared various characteristic of Latin American populism of the time. *Liberacionistas* themselves stressed their ideological brotherhood with European social democratic movements, but perhaps their closest equivalent was Dr. Juan Bosch, first a prominent leader of the opposition to the Dominican dictator Rafael Trujillo and then president himself. During a quarter century in exile, he spent several years in Costa Rica in the 1950s and 1960s and closely collaborated with PLN circles in training party militants. His contributions on Costa Rican history were published in the country with PLN support.[16]

Others who would come to power by coups or armed struggle rather than elections, whether in Bolivia, Venezuela, Cuba, or Nicaragua, found inspiration in Figueres's brief but heroic phase in support of the Caribbean Legion and his pact to overthrow the region's dictators. However, the most outstanding characteristic of later *liberacionista* development was its curious combination of reform and reaction, visible in the expression "reformist anticommunism."[17] There is nothing strange about it, if we take into account the abovementioned confusion over whether Perón and Vargas should be identified with the brownshirts of Mussolini, Hitler, or Franco, or with the red star of Stalin, when they were merely populists wavering between right and left during their careers in power. Social democrats, indeed, from the start, the PLN could be more anticommunist than anti-oligarchic, and vice versa, depending on the context.

The insurrectionary movement that José Figueres and his associates sought to convert into a dominant electoral force rejected not only the legitimacy of *calderonismo* and its electoral methods but also the social bases central to its reformist "brand." Rather than the *calderonista* formula of joining workers, especially banana workers, together with urban popular groups and a sector of public employees and free professionals supportive of the regime, the PLN aimed to mobilize large peasant/rural/farmer majorities of the Central Valley with development policies that would extend the benefits of state action to their communities following its armed victory. To challenge the reformist description when confronting the *calderonista* achievements in favor of unionization and worker rights, along with its improvements in the few cities of the Central Valley, the PLN's competitive reformism would be congruent with its nature from birth, which was reformist and anticommunist. Its own political base would need to guide a process of agricultural modernization, especially in the coffee sector, where the majority of the national population could still be found in the 1950s, together with the creation of multiple institutions capable of impacting their lives. At the same time, it needed to enormously increase the number of positions in the public sector for professionals and managers. These policies generated and consolidated the two most loyal *liberacionista* voting blocs for nearly a half century.

One of the differences between Costa Rican reformisms—between *calderonista* and *liberacionista*—was particularly relevant: farmer participation. As Diane E. Davis has shown in comparing two Asian cases of sustained economic growth (South Korea and Taiwan) with two Latin American cases of recurring crises and stagnation (Argentina and Mexico) between 1950 and 1990, small and midsize farmers played a fundamental role.[18] When the dominant political coalition found support in a multitude of small-scale farmers who were fully incorporated into commercial markets (beneficiaries of profound land reforms following World War II, in the Asian cases), they exercised a disciplining power over state policies, whether democratic or authoritarian. Thus did they avoid the kind of inflation and loss of competitiveness inherent in sectoral pacts negotiated between employers and industrial workers (the formula typical of classic Latin American populism), where costs are transferred to captive consumer markets without a similar check. Moreover, to the extent that markets for agricultural products, whether for local consumption or for export (as with coffee), are highly competitive, they transmit stimuli or checks on production levels much more efficiently than collective bargaining agreements and industrial plans within markets whose prices are permanently distorted owing to protectionism, making them unsustainable and condemned to acute cyclical crises. Needless to say, the agricultural sector is more effective in transferring the benefits of productivity gains to other sectors of the economy, thanks to the direct participation of the majority of the population, than are minority groups of union workers concentrated in one or few cities and without the real possibility of competing via exports in foreign markets. In effect, the deepening of democratic practices depended, in part, on those same democrats accepting market discipline beyond their direct control.

Anticommunist Reformism: From Springtime to Fall

In its historical springtime, Figueres's *liberacionismo* had to confront an earlier tradition of social reform—which it also sought to replace completely. This tradition included not only 1940s *calderonismo* but also the anti-imperialism so deeply rooted in the region, from the national war against William Walker in 1856–1857 to the U.S. interventions in the Caribbean and neighboring Nicaragua and Panama in the twentieth century. Figueres's statement "This is the Yankee imperialism you have heard so much about" is a reflection of that enormous ideological challenge. Employing ironic and sarcastic tones, he sought to redefine national reformism as pro- rather than anti-American. As convincing as that message may have been for the farmers and their family members (soon to be co-op members and loyal *liberacionista* voters) who, in 1948, gathered in Pacayas, Cartago, in front of the new U.S.-sponsored Inter-American Technical Services in Agricultural Sciences—known as STICA, for Servicio Técnico Interamericano de Cooperación Agrícola (figure 1)—such half-truths have infiltrated decades of academic analyses of Costa Rican politics.

In reality, from early on, Costa Rica held a position of honor in the anti-imperialist ranks, thanks precisely to its uncomfortable proximity to Panama and Nicaragua as well as to its own experiences with the United Fruit Company and that company's monopolistic control of the banana industry. During the first three decades of the twentieth century, many prominent Costa Rican intellectuals attempted to join nationalism with important points of the regional and continental anti-imperialist agenda.[19] The high point of its direct influence in politics was undoubtedly the second half of the Calderón Guardia administration (1940–1944) and that of his successor Teodoro Picado (1944–1948), with their alliance with the communist party Vanguardia Popular, prior to their defeat and proscription in 1948. However, one could argue that the broad popularity of ideas central to anti-imperialism was even greater in earlier decades and that this, much more than any fear that the left would recover in the electoral arena, was why the PLN's "organic intellectuals" felt the need,

FIGURE 1. "This is the Yankee imperialism you have heard so much about." President José Figueres Ferrer inaugurating the STICA office in Pacayas, Cartago, 1948. From STICA and the Institute of Inter-American Affairs Food Supply Mission to Costa Rica, *Progress in Agriculture in Costa Rica: Summary Report, 1942–1948* (Washington, DC: Food Supply Division, Institution of Inter-American Affairs, 1949), 18. (Photo courtesy of Wilson Picado)

after their victory in 1948, to systematically and virulently attack any alternative ideological tradition of reformism.

It was not enough to show that *liberacionismo* had achieved broad popular support, especially among farmers in general and those of the Central Valley in particular, sufficient to win elections with overwhelming majorities. To defeat its opponents—the *"calderocomunistas"* of the moment as well the earlier unnamed ideologues of the anti-imperialist tradition—Costa Rican reformism had to be redefined as not just inherently anticommunist but also always ready to defend the virtues of small-scale property and the democratic traditions of its proprietors.

There was no shortage of ironies in that message. Much of the popularization of a quintessential leftist, if not anti-imperialist, idea of the inexorable impoverishment of small farmers at the hands of the "trust" of the coffee processors and of the need for state intervention, from the first law regulating such relations in 1932, came from the writings of the intellectual founders of *liberacionismo* itself, such as Rodrigo Facio and Carlos Monge. As much as the anti-imperialist left might join in the celebratory chorus of condemnation, they were anything but its only composers. The left's electoral support among such farmer populations oscillated violently from the 1920s until its low point during the anticommunist crusades after 1948. In one of the zones closely studied here, Santo Domingo de Heredia, the communists even received 45% of the votes in the parliamentary elections of 1942.[20]

The *calderonista* reforms, the labor code, and the creation of the social security health system, represented neither threat nor relief for small coffee farmers. Neither were they a direct motivation for their mobilization in favor of or against the regime.[21] The labor code and health coverage essentially depended on continuous or permanent wage work, conditions that rarely characterized the seasonal and piecework employment within the small-scale coffee economy. In the agricultural sector, only the tiniest minority had coverage, unlike the banana workers, who had year-round employment and who, not coincidentally, were the only rural or agricultural base of the communist party of the era facing U.S. corporate owners—a far cry from the mythical small farmers of classic *liberacionismo*.

Small farmers, especially in remote colonization zones, were undoubtedly critical participants in the triumphant insurrection of 1948. However, contrary to *liberacionista* reformist teleology, the building of electoral support for the party and for its social democratic vision more generally was entirely a post-1948 process. With such a support base, the PLN could devise both its electoral alliance and an ideological mythology as both the essential and the only legitimate Costa Rican reformist force and tradition.

José Figueres represented an extraordinarily attractive and skillful figure in this process, not only for his impeccable English or his U.S.-born first wife. He was able to successfully navigate rough waters as Cold War polarization deepened. He knew how to use his unquestionable anticommunist credentials, even when his policies and statements in favor of state intervention in the economy infuriated Cold War conservatives and militants equally at home and in Washington. However, it was not until the co-op movement in the coffee economy arose after 1960 that a more profound transformation of Costa Rican society came into view, since it gave real, material content with a distinctive rural flavor to social democratic principles and ceased being a tropical, rhetorical version of the Cold War anticommunist crusade.

For many former *liberacionista* intellectuals, regrouped in the Citizen Action Party after 2002, the waning season of the PLN, marked by its supposed abandonment of social democratic principles and conversion into a center-right force, had a name: Óscar Arias Sánchez, the two-time *liberacionista* president and Nobel Peace Prize winner. Though not everyone expressed their unhappiness so personally, one of the major founders of PAC, and a premier PLN organic intellectual after 1948, Alberto Cañas Escalante, did not mince words, referring many times to the topic. The critique of a rising "*-arismo*" within the PLN pointed to the damage caused by Arias's insistence on achieving a supreme court "reinterpretation" of the prohibition against presidential reelection—in place since 1969—which was declared unconstitutional in his favor in 2003, the promotion of candidates not only loyal to his faction but also much wealthier than in the past, as well as his questionable actions in 2007 in favor of the approval of the referendum on the Central America Free Trade Agreement with the United States.

However, personal resentments disguise more than they reveal about the tectonic processes that better explain the generational, ideological, and socioeconomic transitions the PLN has suffered. In effect, a major part of this book's argument does no more than point to the breadth of the process of social change engendered by the success of the *liberacionista* model of agriculture, in particular, and of national modernization more generally. Even when the analysis is limited to rural or agricultural fields, those who benefited most from the triumphant model, among them our co-op informants, went from a majority to an ever smaller minority, not only in the country but also in the countryside. They were transformed from young entrepreneurs, members of voluntary producer organizations, and heads of families with numerous children, hungry for opportunities and ready to serve as generational replacements, to a radically different situation.

There has been ferocious criticism of the possible motives for the party's turn to the right—the chance to court the votes of the nation's business classes, thanks to the virtual collapse of the PUSC and *calderonismo*; the rise of the evangelical vote; the weight of large amounts of multinational capital within the party's ranks, thanks to the tourism, pineapple, drug trafficking, and money laundering industries; and so on. But these criticisms dangerously disregard the very same social, economic, and demographic evolution of the most traditional *liberacionista* voter base that is the central theme of this book. The lack of self-criticism is not only its own punishment but also another source of misunderstanding, simply in the interest of assigning mythical historical blame rather than confronting actual historical challenges. Beyond assigning blame, and far from the golden age of Figueres and unquestionable *liberacionista* electoral majorities, the campaign manager of the party's current presidential candidate—Antonio Álvarez Desanti—was left to vehemently and anxiously alert his followers to prepare for the challenges of a looming campaign and the likelihood of a second electoral round, since they can no longer count on the 40% of the vote needed to win in the first round.[22]

José Figueres had the first word here, but the last belongs to my enchanting octogenarian interviewee, Rafael Naranjo Barrantes (figure 2), who fought alongside Figueres in 1948 on their shared local turf in Tarrazú. The intense cultivation of a shared social ideology among loyal *liberacionistas* found surprisingly eloquent expression in Rafael's memories. In his youth, he remembered working for the only large coffee processor in the area, Tobías Umaña, as well as processing his limited coffee harvests with him, in the bad old times before the arrival of the roads, the co-ops, and electricity—which soon appeared in rapid succession. His party affiliation in the civil war of 1948 and his lifelong support for the co-ops and the PLN were no secret. However, he also retained strong feelings about the abuses of those faraway times. His contemptuous description of things back then revealingly mix historical time periods and metaphors: "We were in the hands of don Tobías, . . . who paid whenever

FIGURE 2. Don Rafael Naranjo Barrantes at his home in San Marcos, Tarrazú. (Photo by the author)

he wanted and almost whatever he wanted as well. . . . Imagine, they paid in scrip or in merchandise [the overages/remnants of coffee deliveries], as if it were Cuba."[23]

His memory of the system of payment in scrip, usable only in Umaña's commissary in the 1930s and 1940s, was accurate enough, but invoking Castro's Cuba as the most effective denunciation of that neofeudal system, while anachronistic, readily links up with *liberacionista* social democratic ideology, equal parts anticommunist and anti-oligarchic. For those willing to see, the essence of *liberacionismo* was as visible in its springtime as in its fall.

Our Road Map

A reinvigorated social science interest in the agrarian bases of, or obstacles to, democratic development has emerged as neoliberal orthodoxy has collapsed over the past two decades. However, an unfortunate legacy of that brief era of neoliberal hegemony has been the tendency to reduce public debate to a very often simplistic choice between markets and private sector efficiency and the misguided and self-destructive intervention of the public sector. On the one hand is market "discipline," and on the other is "populist" indiscipline and "corruption." The processes by which these same critics benefited from public sector interventions that instructed them in the virtues of new forms of "market discipline" seem very remote. Yet, far from being an exceptional case of preexisting structural determinacy whose democracy could not be replicated elsewhere, Costa Rica's relative success was highly dependent on historical agency, with a healthy dose of public sector intervention to spur rapid productivity and income gains in agriculture.

Beyond purely structural analysis, however, the historical experiences of cooperative coffee farmers, as well as a consideration of their memories and the meanings associated with them, have been elusive. Thus, I have added to the archival data, gathered over more than three decades, some three dozen interviews carried out in 2009, in collaboration with my colleague Wilson Picado Umaña of the Universidad Nacional. These interviews represent the voices of the co-ops' founding generation in Heredia and Tarrazú, as well as of their collaborators among agronomists and agricultural extentionists of the era.

Recognition of the speed and depth of these structural transformations is barely visible in the literature, beyond comments on the "success" of the movement in the mid-twentieth century. I hope that the use of autobiographical materials on historical memory will contribute to the contemporary trend toward a history and social science informed by a series of humanities-derived concepts. The lessons to be learned from such hybrid approaches can contribute to a more historically grounded, heterodox, and comparatively oriented discussion of democratization and agrarian social structures in the future.

The two coffee regions where interviews were recorded (see map) were chosen, in part, based on each researcher's prior experience, and they shed light on the great contrasts within the coffee economy. Santo Domingo and San Isidro, both in Heredia province, were regions that began coffee production early in the nineteenth century. Moreover, their levels of soil fertility and productivity were among the nation's highest and the region's farmers were among the first to support a cooperative (La Libertad, founded in 1960). For its part, the Tarrazú region in the province of

Location of Santo Domingo-San Isidro and Tarrazú in Costa Rica

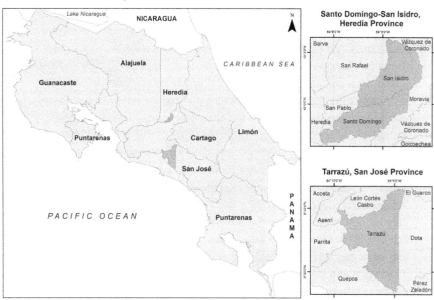

Source: División Territorial Administrativa, scale 1:250000. Instituto Geográfico Nacional.
Cartographic Design: Bepsy Cedeño-Montoya

San José, then a very remote valley far to the south, was also a producer of high-quality coffee and an early partisan of the cooperatives (1960), but its difficult access meant that few of the tendencies toward social differentiation and commercial development visible in Heredia managed to scale the mountains.

Our interview material covered a wide range of concerns, from production techniques and environmental history to the questions of class formation and political loyalties. However, they converged on the portrait of a dense social web of small farmers whose petty bourgeois aspirations were leveraged by allied political forces, not only with the co-op movement but also with the vast expansion of public sector services (education and health, in particular) during the 1960s and 1970s. The dramatic readjustments of the 1980s initially were seen by many as a threat to co-op members' interests, but few realized how these formerly numerous rural families were declining in number as a consequence of their own success, as their ever fewer and better educated children left behind farms and the coffee industry. These older and more privileged groups organized in coffee co-ops proved very capable of defending their interests within the neoliberal order following the collapse of the International Coffee Agreement in 1989. Likewise, they were increasingly unwilling to support—much less to lead—reformist social movements opposed to the antistatist, pro-market, orthodox new order dominant from 1990 forward.

Before fully entering into the analysis of the trajectory of the co-ops' founding generation, we need to get to know their social origins much better. In chapter 2, I present different types of documentation on the forebearers of my Heredia informants, the founders and early members of the La Libertad cooperative, as well as on the first successes of the co-op enterprise. In chapter 3, I change perspective, employing their testimony to explore the fabric of collective memory and its representation of lived historical experience, which found its expression in metaphors, jokes, and ironies. In chapter 4, I offer an analysis of both the cooperatives' processing capacities and the radical changes in the global environment for the marketing and consumption of the "golden bean," from Juan Valdez to Starbucks, from mass consumption to the gourmet era, in the half century following the rise of the coffee co-ops. Finally, in chapter 5, I reflect on the profound transformations of Costa Rican society during that same time period, which was undoubtedly tied to the triumph of the co-ops in the world of coffee. However, these are not always recognized as an integral part of the agricultural and rural modernization process led by the coffee sector, and even less as a consequence of those same decisions, made, consciously or not, by individuals born into families in this new world, which is ever less coffee-based. Thus, my use of the expression "unexpected consequences" in that chapter's title. For me, early twenty-first-century Costa Rica represents the end of a whole model of society and the birth of another: Costa Rica after coffee.

2

Informants and Their Ancestors in Heredia

The Founding Generation in the Census and Probate Records

Beginning in the 1950s, small and medium-size coffee growers in Costa Rica were able to organize a cooperative movement that would profoundly alter the political and social system, first by offering alternative outlets and sources for processing, financing, and marketing, as well as technical assistance, and then by fomenting the dramatic productive advances associated with the conversion to dwarf variety bushes in the 1970s. My first incursion in this field of study, long ago, sought to follow the historical evolution of these small and medium-size coffee operations, so often praised but rarely documented as such, in relatively central regions of Heredia: Santo Domingo and San Isidro.[1] In that work, I managed to document parallel processes of downward social mobility and generalized out-migration of the agricultural population, along with the consolidation of a rural petty bourgeoisie, my stated focus in that study as well as in this one.

Starting from that most recent research, based on interviews done in 2009 with members of the founding generation of the cooperatives and their agronomist and agricultural extensionist allies, this chapter employs information from these interviewees as well as an early list of members of La Libertad cooperative (1971), nearly all of whom were residents of Santo Domingo and San Isidro, to track aspects of their social and family origins as revealed in census and probate records.[2] In effect, this study amounts to an experimental essay designed to see what sorts of results we might achieve by attempting to connect our informants and their fellow co-op members with databases gathered earlier, always with the goal of analyzing class (trans)formation processes based on nominal and longitudinal information. In other words, these are life cycle or life course studies, detailing lived experiences and their transformation into memory and meanings, rather than a purely structural snapshot at one point in time. Thus, my goal has not been and is not the analysis of all the social classes generated by coffee agriculture in zones of rapid urbanization such as these, but rather to document and understand the experience of the ever less numerous surviving coffee farmers. In this way, I seek to get closer to their worldview, their political and organizational positions, and the social transformations generated as a consequence.

Costa Rica's often-invoked "century-old democracy" had little to do with the success of the co-op movement. Rather, this can be explained by their organizational talents and political strategies as well as by the noteworthy material resources of key members. That success, along with the minor and ineffective resistance on the part of affected private processors, can largely be explained by the early participation within the co-ops of rather large nonprocessor growers, some of whom had previously been major suppliers of beans to those processors. Exploring where those talents and resources historically came from illuminates why they had such unusual success not only in surviving but also in leading their own Green Revolution, harvesting its rewards after 1970 in a still very small-scale agricultural system.[3] The impact of such broad agricultural participation in these advances is evident in the deep processes of sociopolitical transformation begun by that generation, with highly visible consequences yet today.

I will begin, then, by briefly describing the types of sources and how they are employed, followed by general comments on the statistical profile and comparisons of the different populations as revealed by those sources. Then I will analyze a few key topics, such as the structure of coffee production and processing over time and the role of the rural "gentry" or local *fuerzas vivas* (active forces) of the small and medium-size bourgeoisie in consolidating the co-op, starting not so much from the interviews but from a great variety of documentary sources.

Beyond the two dozen interviews with Heredia growers, I start with a 1971 list from the co-op La Libertad, which details the names (with both surnames) of its 504 members and the amount of capital investment in the co-op promised and subscribed to that point.[4] Of these 504, I located 78 individuals who were registered in the agricultural census of 1955 as landowners of 1 *manzana* (0.7 hectares) or more, and then traced them back to the population census of 1927. Of the 504 members in 1971, I located 106 individuals in the 1927 census, always with given and both surnames. If I add to these 106 people their family members who declared an occupation (those over fourteen years of age, basically) in the 1927 census, we have a total of 282 people identified. Unfortunately, I located only a dozen or so deceased direct ancestors of the 1971 co-op members in my database of 630 probate inventories for the region between 1840 and 1940. Finally, we have data on the volume of coffee processed in the area by different processors for each annual harvest from 1964–1965 to 2002–2003. After analyzing the statistical profile of these founding generation members, we can explore in greater detail those few topics and cases for which we have multiple and varied information sources, taking full advantage of the interviews recorded in 2009.

Statistical Profiles of a Poorly Lit Coffee Grove

Santo Domingo and its hamlets were called a "poorly lit coffee grove," a moniker assigned to the province of Heredia in jest by one of its favorite native sons. It was one of the most coffee-dominated regions, with the broadest distribution of landed property. In table 1, we can see that in 1935, more than half of the population of Santo Domingo (58.3%) and San Isidro (51.2%) resided on coffee-growing farms. These numbers are higher than in Heredia province in general (49%), and much higher than in San José province (29.9%).

Table 1. Rural Population Residing on Coffee Farms In 1935

Province/District	Percentage
San José	29.9
Highest	71.0
Lowest	6.9
Heredia	49.0
Highest	63.4
Lowest	39.6
Santo Domingo	58.3
San Isidro	51.2

Source: Carlos Merz, "Estructura social y económica de la industria del café en Costa Rica: Estudio estadístico-analítico," *Revista de Instituto para la Defensa del Café* 5, no. 30–38 (April–December 1937): 181.

The broad distribution of property is revealed in different ways in tables 2 and 3. The 1927 census inquired in depth about declarants' occupations—whether *jornalero/peón* (laborer), *cuenta propia* (self-employed), or *dueño/patrón* (owner/employer)—and property ownership. About 40% of the males declaring occupations (age fourteen and older) could be found in the superior categories of *self-employed* or *owner/employer.* Comparing the occupation and property declarations is even more revealing. We find not only the logical association between owner/employer and property ownership but also many cases of male laborers and women (homemakers and daughters) with landed property. We also see that the clear majority of self-employed males lack property ownership.

In effect, many male laborers and female homemakers (*oficios domésticos*) had inherited landed property without being able to dedicate themselves full-time to cultivating it. Likewise, several of our informants disclosed that their entry into the world of coffee growing had been as the person in charge, or administrator, of small properties of older female relatives. This led to contradictory cases of male heads of household registered as if they were owners (*dueños*) of coffee farms, though they were in fact only employers with workers under their control, while also declaring that they owned no land.[5]

Table 2. Male Occupations in 1927

Occupational Category	Santo Domingo (%)			San Isidro (%)		
Laborer, *peón*, etc.	62			57		
Self-employed	21			24		
Owner/employer	17			18		
Total	100			99		
Cases	689			813		
Own Property in 1927	Yes	No	Cases	Yes	No	Cases
Laborer, *peón*, etc.	13	87	430	32	68	467
Self-employed	35	65	144	42	58	197
Owner/employer	77	23	115	86	14	149
Total			689			813

Note: Of the women declaring an occupation (nearly all "domestic" or "own account"), 214 of 791 in Santo Domingo and 136 of 832 in San Isidro also declared property ownership.

Source: 1927 census.

Table 3. Male Heirs in Probate Records and Land Ownership in Santo Domingo, 1927

Occupational Category	Age in 1927 (%)				
	Under 30	30–49	50+	Cases	Percentage
Laborer, *peón*	63	40	34	46	43
Self-employed	30	23	18	24	22
Owner/employee	7	37	48	37	35
Cases in category	27	30	50	107	

Source: 1927 census.

However broadly agricultural property was distributed, the tendency toward downward socioeconomic mobility was equally evident for all residents in the first half of the twentieth century. Over one-third of the population born in Santo Domingo (38.6%) and San Isidro (44%) who were registered in the 1950 population census had emigrated to other regions of the country, a net emigration of 26.5% and 40.4%.[6] Other ways in which this pressure toward relative social class polarization was revealed included the delay of marriage, especially among the landed, with the resulting start of a demographic transition that accelerated radically in the decades from 1960 to 1990.[7] The 1927 census allows us to follow the trail of 107 males found as heirs in probate files (table 3). Of these, 43% appear as "laborers," 34% of whom are over fifty years of age.

Against this complex panorama, what can we say about the social origins of the members of La Libertad in 1971? First, we have the data on each member's capital investment. According to Marco Tulio Zamora Alvarado, each founding member was obliged to invest the value equivalent to two *manzanas* (1.4 hectares) in coffee and to process their harvest with the co-op, risking the loss of that same investment if the co-op were to fail.[8] By 1971, his own investment was a little more than 4,000 *colones* (just over $600). In table 4, we can see that the great majority of members had invested less than Marco Tulio, with a median value of only 2,000 promised and 1,296 already subscribed. Nonetheless, some rather large growers were already participating, with up to 50,000 promised and 38,787 subscribed, although only thirty-three members had pledged 10,000 *colones* or more.

When we trace the 78 members back to the 1955 agricultural census,

Table 4. Capital Promised and Amount Subscribed in La Libertad in 1971 (*colones*)

	Capital Promised			Subscribed		
	Median	*Maximum*	*Minimum*	*Median*	*Maximum*	*Minimum*
504 members	2,000	50,000	90	1,296	38,787	10
106 members in the 1927 census	1,850	50,000	100	1,318	38,787	33
78 members in the 1955 agricultural census	1,000	50,000	100	792	38,787	33

Table 5. La Libertad Members' Ages in 1971 (of Members Identified in the 1927 Census)

Age	*Number*	*Percentage*
40–49	13	12
50–59	30	28
60–69	40	38
70+	23	22
Total	106	100

and some 106 back to the 1927 population census, we find little difference among them in terms of amounts pledged. In other words, even when members identified in earlier sources could be presumed to be older (and perhaps wealthier) than the average member in 1971, they actually declared a smaller average investment. Given the relatively older age distribution (in 1971) of the members traced to the 1927 census (table 5), a possible explanation—and one revealed in several informant interviews—would be the tendency of growers approaching the end of their generational cycle to sell coffee plots or to distribute them as inheritance during their lifetimes. In fact, among the members in 1971 whose age could be calculated based on the 1927 census age declaration, the sixty-three individuals over sixty years of age in 1971 could hardly have found themselves at the high point of their coffee production or land ownership.

The socioeconomic distribution of the members identified in 1927 and 1955 shows very little difference from the rest of the world of coffee locally. If we broaden the comparison to include all the adult family members in

Table 6. Those Declaring Occupations and Members of Their Households (77) in 1927 Identified as Members of La Libertad in 1971 (%)

| | Ages | | | Cases | Percentage |
	Under 30	30–49	50+		
Male members					
Laborer	54	42	—	30	52
Self-employed	35	—	—	16	28
Owner/employer	11	58	—	12	21
Total	100	100	—		
Cases	46	12	—	58	
Property owners					
in 1927	22	50	—	16	28
Female members					
Self-employed	100	100	—	100	
Cases	10	1	—	11	
Property owners					
in 1927	30	—	—	3	27
Male relatives					
Laborer	40	32	10	31	31
Self-employed	50	32	5	35	35
Owner/employer	10	36	85	33	33
Total	100	100	100	99	
Cases	48	31	20	99	
Property owners					
in 1927	10	65	80	45	45
Female relatives					
Laborer	—	2	7	2	2
Self-employed	100	95	93	111	97
Owner/employer	—	2	—	1	1
Total	100	99	100	100	
Cases	56	43	15	114	
Property owners					
in 1927	11	42	33	29	25

Note: In the 1927 census, a total of 282 individuals (typically age fourteen and older) in 77 households declared an occupation; 93 declared real property ownership.

1927 (over age fourteen and thus with occupational and property ownership declarations), we have not just 106 but 282 household members (table 6). A total of 93 declared property ownership—32 women and 61 men. The male occupational declarations almost exactly follow the declarations of the general population, with half of the members of the co-op identified as young laborers in 1927 but only one-third of their "family members" appearing in that category, explainable by the fact that the later co-op members formed a younger group at that moment.

Just as in the general population, 80% of males over fifty owned property, with between one-third and one-half of women over thirty in the same favored property-owning condition. One could say, in effect, that in the world of small and medium-size coffee growers, 75% of males under thirty lacked landed property, between one-half and two-thirds of those between thirty and fifty had gained access to it, and nearly all those over fifty owned property but actually were facing the dilemma of how to organize landed succession for the next generation.

The most important comparative data, without a doubt, comes from the 1955 agricultural census. If we examine the co-op members identifiable therein, we find very few differences with the general distribution of all landowners in the census (tables 7, 8, and 9). Perhaps the only important difference lies in the lower numbers of co-op members among the smallest and largest land owners (table 7). In line with the interviewees' statements, the evidence suggests that the largest growers were reluctant at first, waiting for clear signs of the co-ops' success before changing loyalties for processing their harvests. The absence from the co-ops of growers with more than 20 *manzanas* of coffee is striking here, though that situation was soon remedied, as we will see.

Perhaps equally important to note is the lesser participation of micro coffee growers (*minifundistas*) among members than in the general landed population (for land in coffee, 27% of the general population, compared to 20% of co-op members). Average harvests in *fanegas* (46.2 kilograms) per *manzana* ran parallel to general patterns in 1955 (table 8), just as with the data on the number of seasonal laborers or *cosechadores* (harvesters) (table 9). In both cases, the other notable difference was the relative absence of the largest and the smallest growers compared to the predominance of medium-size farms and coffee plantings. Thus, the basic pattern is reflected over and over again: the co-op preferentially recruited among the middle strata and responded to the needs of the small and medium-size coffee bourgeoisie. It was open to the future incorporation of the poorest and the wealthiest, but it remained anchored in the thickest, most solid section of that "poorly lit coffee grove."

Table 7. Farm Size and Coffee Plantings, Santo Domingo and San Isidro, 1955

Size	Farmers in 1955				Members of La Libertad (1971) in 1955			
(manzanas)	Farm		In Coffee		Farm		In Coffee	
	No.	%	No.	%	No.	%	No.	%
>1.0	75	12	146	27	4	5	15	20
1.1–3.0	192	32	208	38	23	29	26	35
3.1–5.0	80	13	77	14	11	14	16	22
5.1–10	131	22	78	14	24	31	13	18
10.1–20	68	11	24	4	7	9	4	5
20.1+	53	9	11	2	9	12	–	–
Total	599	99	544	99	78	100	74	100
Average					4.5		3.0	

Source: 1955 agricultural census.

Table 8. Coffee Harvest Output in 1955 (%)

Fanegas/Manzana	All Farmers	Members of La Libertad in 1971
1–9.9	70	74
10–14.9	27	24
15+	4	3
Cases	535	76

Source: 1955 agricultural census.

Table 9. Number of Harvest Workers Employed, 1955

| Coffee Farms in 1955 | | Members Identified in 1971 | |
Number	Percentage	Number	Percentage
1–10	76	1–10	66
11–14	14	11–20	25
15+	10	21+	9
(20+)	(7)		
Total	100		100
Cases	600		77

Source: 1955 agricultural census.

Processing Coffee: From the Emergence of the Co-ops to Private/Co-op Equilibrium to Corporate Resurgence

The early success or failure of the co-op movement depended almost completely on its capacity to acquire processing plants and to compete with private processors in attracting members with better prices and conditions. At first, nearly all growers maintained their commercial relationships and coffee harvest deliveries with private processors, whether due to prior commitments, debts, loyalties, or simply as a form of mitigating risk. Several informants commented on the several-year process during which they evaluated their future options. All the informants indicated that their first harvests were delivered to traditional private processors and that they spent several years freeing themselves from both commitments to them and fears of a possible failure of the recently formed co-ops. Others, Gerardo Chacón Chacón in particular, were very clear in revealing that they joined the co-ops relatively late (in the mid-1970s) and remained loyal not as founders or ideological partisans of cooperativism but simply because the co-ops always paid better prices.[9] They did not remember examples of boycotts or threats by their former processors, although at first they feared them. Rather, they remembered how the newfound competition led the private processors to pay better prices and to be more flexible in terms of accepting green coffee or of grading ripe coffee as higher quality.

The speed with which the co-op plants emerged is surprising from any point of view. In a decade, they came to compete with the three dominant private processors in the area (Tournon, Rohrmoser, and Montealegre), and in another decade they exceeded these processors. These three enterprises were founded by a family of French origin (Tournon), by a German (Rohrmoser), and by the last high-profile family dating to the late colonial period (Montealegre), originally resident in San José, site of the greatest concentration and modernization of processing plants to that point.[10] While it is true that these three firms' dominance only increased during the first half of the twentieth century, especially as a consequence of the crisis of the 1930s, it is no less important to note that this process occurred within the historical memory of the socioeconomic actors involved. If it was not all that new, its reversal or possible change was at least conceivable.

Some of the nonprocessor growers, early members of the co-op or not, were descendants of old-time processors, from the rustic "dry" to the small-scale "wet method" plants. Even when the coffee produced in Heredia was very often considered best quality, according to the experts of the time, its processing left a lot to be desired. At the start of the twentieth century, Heredia fell behind the provincial leader, San José, in terms of the consolidation of large-scale processing plants "moved by steam or water with a dryer." This remained true even when the cycles of price depression (1878–1885 and 1896–1910) pushed Heredia's growers in the same direction, toward greater scale, concentration, and perfection of the wet process, distant from the producing farm (table 10). The acceleration of that process in the twentieth century more than equaled the earlier "modernization" of San José, as it went from fifty-three registered plants in Santo Domingo and its hamlets in 1887 to only six in 1935 (five in Santo Domingo and one in San Isidro).[11]

One or another wealthy area resident continued with relatively small plants during the entire twentieth century. For example, the firms of Juan León Villalobos and of Humberto León Hernández continued functioning for decades but went from being competitors of La Libertad in terms of size to processors of volumes barely 10% to 15% of the co-op's output. Small plants more often disappeared, like the firm of Eloy León, which ceased operations after the 1966–1967 harvest, when his processing plant was sold to La Libertad, or that of Amado Sánchez, who sold his La Valenciana plant to the co-op in 1961 and jokingly claimed that, when they were unable to pay the first installment of the mortgage, he would keep their down payment of 300,000 *colones* as a juicy yearly rent.[12] Another proof of the continued consolidation and greater scale in coffee process-

Table 10. Classification of Coffee-Processing Plants by Province, 1900–1910

Province	Class 1	Class 2	Classes 3–4	Total
Alajuela	27	33	18	78
Cartago	39	0	7	46
Guanacaste	3	0	1	4
Heredia	17	21	36	74
San José	47	7	6	60

Note: Class 1: "Moved by steam or water with a dryer"; class 2: "Moved by steam or water without a dryer"; classes 3 and 4: "Without any kind of machinery."

Source: Based on Carlos Naranjo Gutiérrez, "Los sistemas de beneficiado del café costarricense, 1830–1914," *Revista de Historia* 55–56 (January–December 2007), 39–71, figure 1.

ing is the reduction in the number of plants in the country—there were some 115 to 125 in 1975 but 95 to 105 in 1995—precisely during the era of the greatest expansion of harvest volumes.[13]

From the start, the co-op movement was basically split in two in terms of plants and attraction zones for clients. Santa Rosa kept the La Valenciana plant and its clients at lower altitudes, from the Santa Rosa neighborhood toward Santa Bárbara de Heredia. After La Libertad acquired its own processing plant, San Bosco, it concentrated its activities between Santo Domingo and its hamlets and San Isidro, farther up the mountainside. When that plant was no longer able to process all the harvest, La Libertad acquired another, larger one, in San Miguel de Santo Domingo.[14] The neighboring zones produced coffee that the co-op authorities considered "highland grown" and thus of higher quality than that produced by the members of its twin sister, Santa Rosa. This suspicious and implicitly conflictive differentiation helps to explain the early division of the co-op into two—three, in reality—although during its existence, the San Juanillo co-op operated in the same areas and could be considered a subsidiary of Santa Rosa. It figured prominently in the eventual failure of Santa Rosa and San Juanillo in the early 1990s, in the opinion of our informants, though they all were members of La Libertad and perhaps not entirely disinterested witnesses to the case.

Perhaps the best way to document the impact of the rise of the co-ops in terms of coffee processing would be to compare the volume processed by the co-ops with that processed by private and corporate owners, both at the national level and within our study area. At the national level, several tendencies are notable (graph 1). First, we see the continuous growth of the co-op option between 1964–1965 and the early 1980s, when co-ops came to process nearly half of the national harvest. Second, there was a dizzying expansion of national production in the second half of the 1970s, thanks in large part to the conversion to dwarf variety bushes, with which the co-ops could maintain their competitive position. Third, private firms recovered during and after the 1990s, when there were sharp and prolonged price crises, as these actors came to process nearly twice as much coffee as the co-ops; previously, the co-ops were processing as much coffee as all the private options. During this last period, two other factors emerged, which we will discuss in chapter 5: coffee production's displacement toward frontier regions, especially to the south; and the rise of ferocious competition in the world market, which took the form of quality competitions, organic production, origin labeling via patents, and name recognition, sometimes tied to so-called *microbeneficios,* or mini processing plants, specializing in single origin and gourmet varietal schemes of production.

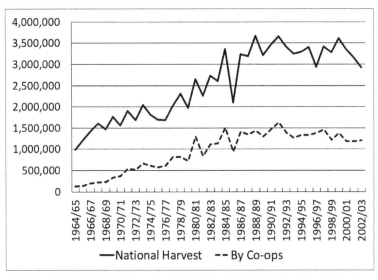

Graph 1. Volume of coffee (*fanegas*) processed nationwide and by co-ops.

Graph 2 compares the two relevant co-ops in the areas of Santo Domingo and San Isidro de Heredia (La Libertad and Santa Rosa) with the three dominant private firms of the time (Tournon, Rohrmoser, and Montealegre). Without exception, our informants identified these three firms as dominant before 1960—Tournon above all. During the 1960s and 1970s, the co-ops were equal to the private firms. During the 1980s, they exceeded the private firms, thanks more than anything to the rapid expansion of operations by Santa Rosa and its affiliate San Juanillo, co-ops that practically ceased to function after the 1990–1991 harvest and went bankrupt definitively by 1993–1994. Although it is true that La Libertad increased its own volume somewhat after the failure of Santa Rosa, the local trend during the 1990s and beyond reaffirms the national trend, although less dramatically, with the recovery of private processing, although not by the three oldest firms. Our informant Carlos Villalobos Chacón joked that the last heiress of the Tournons—"Pascuala So-and-So," he called her—brought her own coffee harvests to the co-op for processing, though this proved aprochryphal.[15] For decades, the Tournon firm continued to be very relevant as a processor within the new co-op scheme of things. The misfortune of its heirs—distant relatives—in recent times turned out to be less important than the earlier collapse of its dominance in the world in which growers like Carlos had developed.

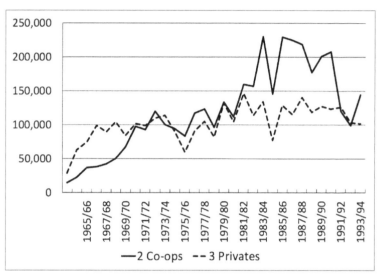

Graph 2. Comparison of coffee (*fanegas*) processing by co-ops and dominant private firms.

The weight of Heredia's production in the national harvest, and that of its two co-ops in particular, varied substantially. In the mid-1960s the two co-ops represented barely 1.5% to 2% of the national total, increasing to 5% to 5.5% between the mid-1970s and early 1980s, then later descending to 2.5% to 3.5% after 1985. As urbanization has advanced in its supplier zones in recent years, the volume processed by La Libertad has fallen substantially, putting at risk the minimum needed to cover its fixed costs (65,000 to 70,000 *fanegas*).[16] The replacement in the national scheme, owing to generalized urbanization of the Central Valley, was felt most in previously peripheral regions of the south (Tarrazú and, above all, San Isidro de El General and Coto Brus) and in western Alajuela (Naranjo), coincidentally the areas that every year compete for the national prize for the highest-quality coffee.[17]

Founders as Exemplars: From Four Paupers to Active Forces

Of my informants, Marco Tulio Zamora Alvarado (figure 3)—surely one of the most eloquent—was the only one among the true founders of La Libertad cooperative. In one of his many suggestive comments about that adventure, he pointed to the limited wealth of the first co-op members, including himself ("We were four paupers"), as well as to the irony that he was "poor" kin of the "richest" major coffee growers in the area, the owners of the so-called Hacienda Zamora, who were initially against the organizing campaign.[18] I heard several times these same expressions ("poor" or "the poor side") from those (out of my fewer than twenty total informants) with kin ties to the Zamoras. In a way, then, the task before us is to explain how it was that, in a single decade, some of the wealthy Zamoras were also to be found among the members of La Libertad. Or, in more general terms, how was it that some of the largest growers decided to change loyalties in favor of the co-op? Marco Tulio's testimony sheds light on many different topics, as we will see, but on this point other perspectives arise from descendants of five key, preeminent, and broadly influential families in Santo Domingo and San Isidro: Barquero, Chacón, Rodríguez, and Villalobos, in addition to Zamora.[19] These families are found among the most overrepresented in the ranks of the propertied, including the largest owners (table 11).

Table 11. Five Paternal Surnames Overrepresented among the Propertied (%)

Paternal Surname	1846	1927SD	1927SI	Probate	1955	1971
Barquero	1.4	2.7	1.6	3.7	4.5	5.4
Chacón	6.4	5.2	2.6	3.8	6.4	3.2
Rodríguez	3.2	4.6	2.8	7.6	6.0	4.8
Villalobos	4.9	7.5	2.7	9.9	9.4	7.9
Zamora	4.1	5.2	1.3	3.5	7.6	3.8

Sources: 1846: population census; 1927SD: population census of Santo Domingo; 1927SI: population census of San Isidro; Probate: 630 cases, from 1840 to approximately 1940; 1955: agricultural census of 603 property owners; 1971: 504 members of the La Libertad cooperative.

ZAMORA, "POOR AND RICH"

In the 1927 census, I found the father of my informant Marco Tulio, Amadeo Zamora Azofeifa (1900–1960), as a twenty-six-year-old male head of household, a landowning coffee farmer beginning his family life with his twenty-three-year-old wife, Rosa Alvarado Arce, and their barely year-old son, Rogelio. Amadeo appears again in the 1955 agricultural census as the owner of 32 *manzanas* of land, 16.5 in coffee, producing 144 *fanegas* with sixteen seasonal laborers. Rogelio Zamora Alvarado was a co-op member in 1971, with 4,048 *colones* subscribed of the 5,000 promised, and he appears as a landowner in 1955 with 10 *manzanas,* with no coffee planted but with two seasonal laborers. His younger brother, Marco Tulio, appears as a member of La Libertad in 1971, with 4,553.60 *colones* subscribed, though only 4,000 were promised. Several individuals with the same surnames, perhaps his relatives, also appear: Edgar, Irma, and Luz María Zamora Alvarado, each with between 3,000 and 5,000 *colones* subscribed, as well as Casta and Emma Zamora Azofeifa, the latter the sister of Amadeo, appearing as subscribers of La Libertad in the same 1971

FIGURE 3. Don Marco Tulio Zamora Alvarado in his yard. (Photo by the author)

list. Emma Zamora Azofeifa (widow of García) had subscribed 6,028 of the 9,000 *colones* promised to the co-op in 1971 and appeared in 1955 as the owner of 28 *manzanas* of land, 8 in coffee, with a harvest of 90 *fanegas* with eight seasonal laborers.

Marco Tulio's father, Amadeo, passed away the same year La Libertad was founded (1960) and never was a member. Marco Tulio recalled one uncle (whom he did not name) who was an early participant in the organizing campaign and faced skepticism and indifference, if not open opposition, from the rest of the better-positioned relatives. Actually, members of this branch of the Zamora family (Zamora Azofeifa and Zamora Alvarado) were not exactly "poor," even though they self-identified this way, in contrast to the heirs of the Hacienda Zamora.

The only co-op member coming from the "rich" Zamoras of the time, the Zamora Chacón branch—the children of Procopio Zamora Chacón and Orfilia Chacón Vargas—was Rogelio Zamora Chacón, subscriber of 37,812.75 of the 40,000 *colones* promised, the second largest supporter among the 504 members. In 1955, Rogelio was the owner of 33 *manzanas* of land, 18 in coffee, harvesting 170 *fanegas* with eleven laborers. His mother, Orfilia, appears in the 1955 census with 7 *manzanas* of land, without coffee; as did Rogelio's siblings, Nereo Zamora Chacón (with 43 manzanas, 30 in coffee, harvesting 370 *fanegas* with thirty-nine harvesters), Lilly Zamora Chacón de Fonseca (with 50 *manzanas*, 27 in coffee, harvesting 125 *fanegas* with twenty-six laborers), and Eida Zamora Chacón de Rodríguez (with 28 *manzanas*, 23 in coffee, harvesting 150 *fanegas* with thirty-seven laborers); and their aunt by marriage, Consuelo Zamora Campos (with 7 *manzanas*, 6 in coffee, harvesting 70 *fanegas* with seven laborers).

Other Zamora Chacóns, their cousins—children of Rodrigo Zamora Chacón and Dominga Chacón Azofeifa—figure among the most distinguished landowners. They were led by Dora, owner of 62 *manzanas*, 50 in coffee, harvesting 500 *fanegas* with forty-five harvesters, and Marjorie, with 30 *manzanas*, all in coffee, harvesting 300 *fanegas* with forty-six harvesters. The "Zamora Commons" of colonial times, transformed into the Hacienda Zamora in the mid-nineteenth century, still represented the pinnacle of Santo Domingo's social pyramid, and the early participation of Rogelio Zamora Chacón as a member of La Libertad proved vitally important.

We can be certain of the kin relationship between Rogelio and the first three Zamora Chacóns because in the 1927 census they are listed as members of a household that is of particular interest for our purposes. I found Rogelio in the home of his parents, José Procopio Zamora Chacón and Orfilia Chacón Vargas, with the three siblings mentioned—Nereo, Lilly, and Eida. His uncle Teodorico Zamora Chacón lived in the house next door with his wife, Consuelo Zamora Campos, and nine individuals between the ages of one and twenty-one with the surnames Zamora Zamora, Zamora Ulate, and Zamora Campos, plus five non-Zamora dependents. A household made up of no less than sixteen individuals was very unusual in a town such as Santo Domingo in 1927. Both heads of household—José Procopio and Teodorico—together with their siblings Graciliano, Nereo, and Aurelia, had in 1920 divided an inheritance upon the death of their mother, Rudesinda Chacón Lizano (1838–1918), widow of Bernardino Zamora García (1833–1884).[20] The property totaled some 50 hectares in nineteen different plots, the majority in coffee, valued overall at 84,591 *colones*. Although this was a case of great import for the coffee industry, no coffee processing plant was listed, only coffee groves, sugarcane, and pastures.

BARQUERO

Another coffee grower who supported the founding of La Libertad from the start was Célimo Barquero Rodríguez (1904–1985), according to his son (and our informant), Orlando Barquero Barquero (figure 4), twice a board member of the co-op. However, three or four years after the co-op was founded, he was still delivering most of his harvest to his old private processor, Tournon, to pay off debts. Célimo appears in the 1927 census as a twenty-two-year-old young man, self-employed as an owner of a coffee farm and living with his parents, Víctor Barquero Vargas (1875–1947), a fifty-year-old owner of a coffee farm, and Adelina Rodríguez Villalobos (1879–1933), a forty-six-year-old, together with his siblings Heriberto (nineteen), Edwin (six), Esperanza (twelve), and Flor María (two). Célimo is listed in the 1955 census as the owner of 18 *manzanas* of land, 17 in coffee, harvesting 144 *fanegas* with forty-four harvesters. Célimo appeared to be one of the most powerful members of the co-op in 1971, with 33,768 *colones* subscribed of the 37,700 promised.

Orlando Barquero Barquero was born in 1946, and just like his siblings, he was able to join the co-op with his father as sponsor as soon as he had

FIGURE 4. Don Orlando Barquero Barquero in his living room. (Photo by the author)

harvested coffee to deliver—no doubt from the land he administered for his sister, even before he owned land. One way or another, all of Orlando's eight brothers and sisters passed through the world of coffee, starting by taking care of small plots destined to be their inheritance. Thus, the first plot that Orlando was in charge of was two *manzanas* assigned to his already married sister. He had his first harvest from land of his own when he was twenty-four, in 1970–1971. Célimo died in 1985 and Orlando has followed the trend of all the others, reducing his coffee business and selling some of the land for building lots.

CHACÓN

If the best way to avoid downward mobility owing to land division in inheritance in Santo Domingo during the second half of the nineteenth century was emigration to Alajuela, to the west, the Chacón family employed the strategy in reverse. According to my informant, Gerardo Chacón Chacón (figure 5), in the 1830s his ancestors emigrated from Naranjo, Alajuela—the favorite destination of Santo Domingo's later emigrants—to Santo Domingo. During the following century, they managed to build one

FIGURE 5. Don Gerardo Chacón Chacón in his living room. (Photo by the author)

of the most solid coffee operations in the area, and they even built a stately house in 1893, where he lived alone when I interviewed him in 2009.

In the 1955 agricultural census, I found Gerardo's father, José María Chacón Chacón, the owner of some 13.2 *manzanas* of land, 7 in coffee, harvesting 50 *fanegas* with thirteen laborers, as well as his uncle Gerónimo, with 7 *manzanas,* 5 in coffee, producing 70 *fanegas* with five seasonal laborers. As a souvenir of those days, he gave me a rustic coin with which they used to pay the harvesters, stamped with his father's initials. The sixty to seventy local harvesters who used to receive those metal coins in his father's day are only a memory today; like all his neighbors, Gerardo has moved to employing only seasonal laborers, not from the area, for the harvest.

Of the group of five brothers of Gerardo's generation, three worked in coffee, but by 2009 he was the only one left, and without children of his own. At the high point, in the 1970s, the brothers achieved harvests of up to 1,200 *fanegas,* but now Gerardo produced only 400 to 500 *fanegas.* Gerardo had renovated his coffee bushes with the dwarf variety Caturra in the decade from 1975 to 1985, growing his own seedlings to reduce costs.

He looked to the co-op to process his coffee, and at times to sell him seeds, but he financed it all on his own account.

RODRÍGUEZ

Perhaps the most critical source for understanding the transformation process in coffee cultivation, particularly with the introduction of the Caturra variety in the 1970s, was Román Rodríguez Argüello (figure 6). Not only did he join the co-op rather late, as was typical of coffee families of a certain gravitas, but also he was a pioneer in the planting and commercialization of Caturra seedlings among his neighbors. Together with two officers of the local technical agricultural assistance office (Servicio Técnico Interamericano de Cooperación Agrícola—figure 7), Carlos Norsa and Segismundo Bolaños, Román built an enterprise that produced some 130,000 seedlings on rented lands close to the Juan Santamaría International Airport. The conversion to Caturra allowed for a planting density more than twice the previous norm, with harvests increasing from some 15 *fanegas* per *manzana* to 30 to 40, once the bushes matured.

FIGURE 6. Don Román Rodríguez Argüello and his wife, Doña Alicia Alvarado Zamora, in their yard. (Photo by the author)

FIGURE 7. Former STICA office in Heredia. (Photo by the author)

In the 1927 census, I found Román's grandfather, Clímaco Rodríguez Alvarado (1870–1944), a fifty-seven-year-old owner of a coffee farm and head of household, with his fifty-five-year-old wife, Rafaela Sáenz Bolaños (1873–1966). Three Rodríguez Sáenz children were listed in this household, Rafael (twenty-eight), Gabriel (twenty-four), and Luisa (nineteen), the two males being self-employed coffee farmers. Román's father, Gabriel, does not appear in the 1955 agricultural census, but according to his son he had some 20 *manzanas* in coffee. Gabriel's mother, Rafaela, does appear, with 16 manzanas of land, 8 in coffee, harvesting 88 *fanegas* with eleven harvesters. According to Román, his father died at the age of ninety-nine, early in the twenty-first century.

In his best years, Román harvested up to 1,500 *fanegas,* but by 2009 he delivered barely 100 to 150, because owing to health problems he had sold land and because, as with so many others of the following generation, his only son (Rodríguez Alvarado) had no interest in coffee. Román's wife, Alicia Alvarado Zamora, was the granddaughter of Graciliano Zamora Chacón, but she self-identified as from the "poor" Zamoras. I found Graciliano in the 1927 census, a fifty-five-year-old owner of a coffee farm, together with his fifty-year-old wife, Laurentina Chacón González, a property owner as well, with their thirty-year-old son Rodrigo Zamora

Chacón, a self-employed farmer, and two domestic servants, twenty and twelve years of age.

VILLALOBOS

If the Zamoras and Chacóns dominated the hamlets southeast of Santo Domingo, the same was true of the Villaloboses higher up the mountain in San Isidro. Their visible overrepresentation in table 11 actually underestimates the families' weight in land ownership and coffee production. In the 1955 census, Villalobos was the first surname of no fewer than ten of the 121 proprietors (8.2%) of more than 10 *manzanas* of land, and of five of the thirty-five (14.3%) with more than 10 *manzanas* in coffee.

Among so many Villaloboses in the area are to be found families of more modest means, like the one headed by my informant Carlos Villalobos Chacón (figure 8). His experience reveals in detail the multiple paths of access to property and coffee production for those less favored by the good fortune that so characterized the Villalobos clan. I found his father, Carlos Villalobos Villalobos (1900–1963), in the 1927 census as a twenty-six-year-old property owner, head of household, but working for

FIGURE 8. Don Carlos Villalobos Chacón in his living room. (Photo by the author)

another on a coffee farm. He was living with his twenty-one-year-old wife, Margarita Chacón Esquivel de Villalobos, and two children, Sara María (one) and Fernando (an infant), in addition to his sister-in-law, Pacífica Chacón Esquivel, a seventeen-year-old property owner. Carlos senior appears in 1955 with 8 *manzanas* of land, 3 in coffee, harvesting 18 *fanegas* with ten harvesters. The wife of the younger Carlos, María del Rosario Villalobos Campos, joined La Libertad early, in 1963 or 1964, and appears in 1971 with 1,910.95 *colones* subscribed of the 2,100 promised.

Carlos had nine siblings—five sisters and four brothers—only one of whom was a co-op member and coffee grower. After marrying in 1956, he began in coffee by caring for plots owned by his great aunt. Then he acquired plots of his own but continued with several occupations he had pursued before he married: in construction (he built his own house), as a clerk in his father's corner grocery in San Miguel, but above all as a milkman, with a daily delivery route for more than two decades.

At first, he delivered his coffee harvests to Tournon, "as everyone here did," but he joined the co-op in 1974 and counted on its loans against harvests to manage the transition to Caturra, and even to buy land in the mid-1970s. He achieved harvests of up to 280 *fanegas,* having begun as a microgrower producing only 4 or 5 *fanegas.* With a pickup purchased in 1958 or 1959, his profits from the milk delivery route allowed him to expand his activities, leaving on his route at three a.m. and working in his coffee groves after one in the afternoon. After twenty-two years of this grueling routine, he was able to retire from the milk delivery route in 1980.

Now that we know better the origins and challenges of the founding generation of the coffee cooperatives, we will change perspective in chapter 3, looking closer at the way in which they recall and represent that collective experience. As a small and medium-size bourgeoisie in formation, they went from marginal in Costa Rica's social and political scene to central to marginal again—all in a single generation. Extracting meanings from such dizzying and disorienting changes, their memories of the past mix with more recent events in a series of metaphors, jokes, and judgments that reveal not just a lived experience but also a world transformed.

3

Green Revolutions and Golden Beans

The Founding Generation's Memories and Metaphors

As the reader will have noticed in chapter 2, an enormous amount of written or archival documentary material exists for Heredia's coffee districts. All my previous research on pre-1950 coffee culture was based entirely on this type of sources. The highly structuralist concerns of social and economic history were as prominent in that work as in the vast literature on the history of coffee cultivation in Latin America and the world beyond.[1] Likewise, large numbers of social science researchers have been drawn to the Costa Rican case precisely in order to understand the roots and processes of democratization, nearly always privileging structural analysis.[2]

Beyond these strategies and documentary sources, other analysts have contributed to the search for the "causes" or conditions for the deepening of democratic practices by using life histories and testimonies.[3] Surprisingly, these sources have been little used for the Costa Rican case, either in the field of historiography or in many others. Three monographs on coffee co-ops and their histories in Costa Rica employ interview material, but essentially as evidence about past events or data on present patterns rather than in search of meanings and interpretations encoded in their informants' memories and metaphors.[4]

In an effort to better understand not only the events of the era but also how they have been represented and interpreted in the memory of their actors, we have interviewed in detail nearly three dozen farmers of the coffee co-op founding generation, as well as the county extentionists and agronomists who worked with them in Heredia and Tarrazú during the key decades from the 1960s to the 1980s, when they achieved major advances in harvests and coffee productivity as well as in farmers' incomes. While the central empirical question of this new research is the social impact of the mid-twentieth-century introduction of new technology in agriculture (including chemical fertilizers, new practices to control soil erosion, and most important, dwarf variety bushes), its findings also seek to illuminate a particular social group's shared "narrative" or "transcript," hidden or not. Such an approach is very common today in both humanities and social science research, begun not only with the linguistic turn of the late 1980s but also used in agrarian classics such as James Scott's *Weapons of the Weak*.[5]

Between 1950 and 1980, Costa Rica outdistanced its neighbors in coffee farm output. In fact, it actually achieved world-leading levels in productivity on what, by any comparative measure, were very small, average coffee farms.[6] Not coincidentally, this was achieved simultaneously with the formation of coffee producer cooperatives, which offered crop processing facilities in competition with formerly dominant private processors. State intervention during the 1950s and 1960s was concentrated in the nationalization of the banking system and in the provision of targeted credit to agriculture via the co-op structure. Only later, during the 1970s, did the dwarf variety bushes make their appearance locally.

The analysis of these memories and metaphors presented here is organized into three sections:

1. The ways in which informants who lived during those difficult yet exciting times remember the class relations and conflicts that led to formation of the co-ops in the 1960s.
2. The memory of the market innovations and production technique transformations of the 1960s and 1970s that allowed for the successful consolidation of the co-ops and their members.
3. Four recurrent informant expressions or metaphors that point to the profound and many times ironic sense of the sources and limits of their historical success.

Cold War Class Struggles: Through a Glass Darkly

The politics of social reform at the height of the Cold War were extraordinarily convoluted in the Costa Rica of the 1940s through the 1970s, and their memory and positioning today are no less so. The single informant who participated as an adult, Marco Tulio Zamora Alvarado, an independent farmer and founding member of the co-op in Heredia, remembers how, as he put it, there was a *"sentida necesidad"* (felt need) among local coffee farmers for the cooperative, as the private processors and lenders had them *"bien exprimidos"* (well squeezed) so long as they had no other options via the co-op processing plants and financing.[7] The entirety of his father's and his own first coffee crop was delivered to the processing plants of the nineteenth-century French immigrant family Tournon, where he also worked as a truck driver during the harvest. His greatest fear, early on, was that the co-op would fail and he would lose his subscription investment, the equivalent of two *manzanas* (1.4 hectares) of coffee land. They all anticipated the opposition of the private processors, and they were not disappointed, but the first sign of their victory was when the processors began to show more flexibility in accepting green coffee for processing, without downgrading its quality so severely as in the past. Even though he was a kin relation of one of those same and much criticized private processors, he described himself and his co-op founders as *"cuatro pelados"* (four paupers) who much resented his own kinsman's haughty closing of the gates of the Hacienda Zamora, effectively closing a public road to those whose organizational activities they opposed.

The common class interests of small and medium-scale coffee farmers were clearly the basis for the co-op's appeal, but the way in which such class interest–based appeals were made, and the way they are remembered today, defies any easy categorization. Those who seek—consciously or not—to remember those days in the classless, rural development mode of progress and improvement for all have no shortage of quite compelling images. To call someone a small or medium-scale farmer in Heredia, the heart of the oldest and wealthiest coffee district, may have implied a good deal of class differentiation and polarization, but in relatively isolated Tarrazú, virtually anyone might imagine themselves as included in this group. A late 1950s photo (figure 9) shows mostly barefoot farmers attending one of the earliest coffee co-op organizing meetings, which was led by an extension agent and attended by the local priest, Rodrigo Jiménez López (seated in the front row, third from the left), a major proponent of the effort, who had arrived in 1954 and is one of the few participants wearing shoes.

Favored workers with far greater access to cash incomes, also shown barefoot, in a 1937 photograph at the *beneficio* (coffee mill) owned by

FIGURE 9. Organizing meeting of the co-op in San Marcos de Tarrazú, late 1950s. (Photo courtesy of Carmen Kordick)

virtually the only local employer, Tobías Umaña, reinforced the same point (figure 10). Prior to the co-op era, even local farmers thought to be "wealthy" enough in land and food security to risk planting coffee remained far removed from the income and consumer culture of the 1970s, when shoes and Sunday clothes were less the markers of success than household appliances and, eventually, vehicles.

Targeting the locally prestigious, independent farmer—the declared strategy of both the co-op organizers and county extension agents—still meant targeting the barefooted, in Tarrazú. If farmers whose production techniques and harvest results were most admired could be won over to the idea of a co-op, others would follow their positive example, rather than responding to proselytizing alone. To ensure that working farmers were involved, co-op organizers moved their meetings from the daytime and the park or schoolyard to after work hours and the local movie theater, the only building in town large enough and with a generator for electric lighting. They also learned to strictly limit the meetings, both so that farmers' daybreak-to-dusk work routines would not be unduly compromised and so that discussions might continue afterward over a drink or two, solidifying any positive messages in small-group formats anchored in the male

FIGURE 10. Workers in Don Tobías Umaña's coffee processing plant in Tarrazú, 1937. (Photo courtesy of Carmen Kordick)

bonding rituals of bars and cantinas. Only there could the leadership by example and results arguments of those successful farmers who favored not only co-ops but also new ways of terracing and planting win over the wavering among the barefoot meeting attendees.[8]

Yet another well-grounded set of images that downplay any specifically class-based or divisive appeal have to do with the ways in which the history of the coffee co-ops defies any simply partisan identification in their origins and dovetails with contemporary movements for both rural electrification and the provision of other local public services. The arguments against partisan identification seem, on the surface, both ironic and lacking in credibility, given the co-op movement's and coffee zone voter support for the PLN over the second half of the twentieth century.

In Tarrazú, at least, support for the 1948 insurrection was nearly universal, given that the armed movement's leader, José Figueres Ferrer, was the region's major employer (along with Umaña, the local coffee magnate). Any historical memory of a pitched battle over the co-op reforms, then, flies in the face of the seemingly more important historical "fact" of local landlords' sharing in the violent opposition movement that led Figueres and the PLN to power.

Moreover, those who lived through the civil war era remember a whole series of events that poorly fit the simple "us versus them" framework for the history of the co-ops and partisan politics. The state-owned Banco Nacional predated both the civil war and the universal bank nationalization of 1949. It created a cooperative division in 1953, long before the coffee co-ops emerged, and its earliest projects were the national dairy co-op (Dos Pinos) and supervising employee-based savings and loan associations. The labor code of 1943 had established that any worker association must have at least twenty members, and this requirement was simply applied to co-ops as well.[9]

The Banco Nacional's co-op division sent abroad for training key figures such as Eduardo Villalón González. A graduate of the Catholic high school (Colegio Seminario) in San José, Villalón studied for the priesthood for an additional three years before leaving the seminary to take a job with the Banco Nacional. The decision to send Villalón to Canada was taken not in response to the PLN efforts of the first Figueres administration (1953–1958) but near the end of the first opposition (anti-PLN) administration to win election after the civil war, headed by President Mario Echandi (1958–1962).

Villalón would return to work in the bank's still very small (only three or four employees in 1962) cooperative division, until it was closed in 1973 as part of a reorganization and merger into the new National Cooperative Institute (INFOCOOP). There followed a much closer (and in Villalón's view, damaging) identification with the PLN administrations of Figueres (1970–1974) and of Daniel Oduber (1974–1978), which were dominated by university-trained economists who viewed co-ops skeptically. As Villalón noted, "They should be seen like (any other) enterprise . . . even though they did not know what a co-op was, or headed departments, since they had never worked in anything like that." Still, Villalón continued to work within the INFOCOOP structure until 1980, when he assumed a key role in the Tarrazú co-op as well, serving as its executive director for a year after it nearly collapsed due to self-indulgent consumerist and risky commercial practices in the boom days of the late 1970s.

Rural electrification co-ops were formed almost immediately after the coffee co-ops in more remote areas like Tarrazú (where such a co-op was founded in 1968), often tapping the same individuals as board members, ensuring once again that "community" or "rural development" rationales would take precedence over polemical or class-based ones in historical memory.[10] The importance of these "safe" appeals to social democratic ideals in the midst of the Cold War can hardly be overstated, as such appeals softened the socialist or "pink" aspects of reformism as critically in 1960s Costa Rica as they had earlier in the New Deal United States.[11]

The linking of these three reforms is reflected in the life experience of one such informant, Noé López, who moved to Tarrazú from Cartago as a twenty-five-year-old in 1951 to work for the Banco Nacional branch office, which already owned a small processing plant that it would later sell to the newly formed co-op in 1960.[12] By the time he retired in 1984, after rising through the ranks to the directorship of the branch office (1970–1984), he had played a key role not only in the coffee co-op's development but also in the rural electric co-op's simultaneous success, serving on its board from the start of its subscription campaign in 1965 to the inauguration of electric lighting in 1969. His own sense of a career arc radically privileges local community development over any form of political partisanship.

Others, however, do remember appeals to deep-seated social and economic resentments, at times in oddly formed but telling associations, at other times in memories of their youth, where humor disguises partisan politics and irony trumps anger and emotion. Perhaps none had the expressive genius of Rafael Naranjo from Tarrazú (figure 2), with his simultaneous denunciations of the local oligarchy and Castro's Cuba, but neither did they lack that moral judgment and feeling of (in)justice on many other accounts. In Heredia, where social and economic differences were far more sharply felt and processors were as often national political leaders as immigrant investor families, the class-based appeals had to be equally sharp for the co-op movement to gain traction. Here, the poorer among the coffee farmers were more likely to be part-time truck/pickup drivers or wage laborers than barefoot corn and bean growers with a milk cow and chickens in the backyard. Several informants invoked images of the Tournon family, one of the most dominant grower/processors of the time, both to remember the heady days of the struggle to create their co-op in 1960 and to reflect on its historic victory amid so many difficulties.[13]

The campaign to organize the La Libertad co-op in Heredia had to confront the power and influence of the private processors, and Tournon was clearly the largest among them. Rather than resorting to any xenophobic appeals, which were unlikely to succeed in any event, given the French family's presence in Costa Rica over many decades (unlike German vulnerability during World War II, for example), co-op organizers sought to focus on material conditions, pure and simple. Jorge Villalobos of San Isidro in Heredia enjoyed recounting how he had once heard the PLN activist and Catholic priest Benjamín Núñez harangue him and his fellows at an early, very small organizational meeting.[14] A leader of the pro-Figueres, anticommunist forces within the Catholic Church before and after 1948, Núñez was also the founding rector of the former teacher's college turned Universidad Nacional in the 1970s, in nearby Heredia. Despite his anticommunist credentials, or precisely because of them, in the 1960s and 1970s Núñez would become the most visible exponent of a left-liberal version of the PLN's social democratic ideology and something of a lightning rod for those disposed to remember a particularly combative version of the co-op creed in its foundational moment. Villalobos remembered that Núñez appealed to a sense of parental obligation (and shame?), supposedly goading his listeners to action with the following example: "You know how the Tournons' [watch]dogs sleep on matresses [*colchones*]? They sleep better than you and with your money. And if one day you see those dogs eating, right, they eat better than you, with your labor, think about it!" Villalobos's father-in-law saw the light and said, "These are my children here and I want to approve the formation of the co-op."

There is a certain joy in remembering a youthful brush with the "famous" and a daring form of political appeal—danger without the risks associated with having to choose, given his youth and lack of property at the time. Whether Padre Núñez uttered those exact words or not, and to whom, is much less the issue here than their being remembered as congruent with his subsequent political profile and legacy. A far more ironic and less politically charged image of the passing of the Tournons' hegemony was provided by our informant Carlos Villalobos, an early co-op member in Heredia. After recounting his work back then as a seasonal truck driver for the Tournons, he delighted in making his sardonic claim about the clan's current heiress, Pascuala, delivering her own coffee to the co-op, an exceedingly rare and delicious irony of complete role reversal.

Markets and Public Policies: Remembering Pathways to Prosperity

While the Costa Rican state took an early interest in both coffee research and regulating conflictive relations between producers and processor/exporters, it was not until the vigorous expansion of the pool of the local equivalent of county extension agents in the 1950s and 1960s that land and labor productivity began their extraordinary increase, reaching world leadership by 1980. This expansion was fed by a number of factors. The increased training of agronomists by the Universidad de Costa Rica's newly formed faculty, the modeling of county extension–like efforts (clearly based on United States and Canadian models, including the 4-H movement) by agents with high school or postsecondary studies but not a university or agronomy degree, and the newfound concern with soil conservation goals all contributed to a substantial improvement in results in the coffee economy prior to the 1970s. However, it was during the decade following 1970 that the key, radical change in coffee's cultivation scheme occurred, with the systematic introduction of Caturra, a dwarf variety. One pioneer in the seedling business estimated that he was able to increase the density of plantings from roughly 1,100 or 1,200 bushes per *manzana* to 4,000 or 5,000 bushes, with harvest volumes more than doubling on the same land area.[16]

Our understanding of this transformation has been enriched by the perspectives of pioneer extension agents, agronomists, and, in particular, coffee farmers involved in the earliest adoption of what could be called "best practices." Lengthy interviews involved topics ranging from the initial drive to create a co-op alternative to private processing and lending practices, to soil conservation techniques and coffee nursery seedling businesses, to one informant's leaving a tenured agronomy professorship in order to "come home" to grow coffee. His extreme form of best practice via career change did not go unrewarded.

While most informants dwelled on the struggles to recruit new members when the co-ops were first formed, given the financial and social risks they faced, it was just as hard to imagine in retrospect how they could acquire and staff the processing plants themselves, the sine qua non of their existence and appeal. Many of the earliest successful co-ops, such as La Libertad and Tarrazú, both founded in 1960, emerged not during the first presidency of their primary historical and electoral allies, Figueres and the PLN, but under his successor, Mario Echandi (1958–1962), when one might well have expected a good deal more conservative opposition and even repression. Within the post-1949 nationalized banking system that would provide the initial support for the co-ops, there had long existed both PLN and non-PLN figures. The non-PLN figures had themselves pioneered the co-op initiatives, sending personnel abroad for training. If they hoped to advance their careers after the 1948 civil war, they had every reason not to oppose the coffee co-op expansion that was so central to Figueres and the PLN's programs in search of both growing farm incomes and popular electoral support.

In Heredia, the process is remembered as both tension-filled and conflictive, and as a surprisingly straightforward commercial transaction. Once the co-ops had enrolled their minimum of twenty members, they could qualify for loans from the nationalized banking system, and their first priority was the acquisition of a processing plant or *beneficio*. Realistically, they needed at least several dozen founding members with harvests sufficient to utilize the processing plant they were purchasing. Their goal was not to rival the size and scope of the private sector, or even of the largest private processor, but to ensure that their members had an alternative outlet for their crop at higher prices and, perhaps most important, to provoke more competitive pricing policies on the part of the remaining private processors.

In other contexts, such challenges might well have been responded to with bloodshed. Two key policies and trends in the Costa Rican coffee economy in the early 1960s worked to limit any overt conflict or sabotaging of the co-op campaigns, even when the administration in power (until 1962, and then again in 1966–1970) was highly identified with the largest private processors. Since the early 1930s, the government had created marketing boards on which nonprocessors would have representation, and legal limits on interest rates and processing charges in coffee export sector transactions, thus muting both conflict and any attempt to exclude small producers from a detailed knowledge of the workings of the export trade.

Ironically, a key boost for the co-op effort came from the ongoing process of depressed prices and consolidation within the industry, which continued to eliminate many small and medium-size processing plants. In effect, there were marginal or recently closed plants available for sale to and expansion by the co-ops, along with trained technical personnel willing to run them rather than face unemployment. Further irony can be found in the fact that some local processors (and even one pioneer co-op, the sugar mill of La Victoria, in western Alajuela province) benefited unscrupulously from the confiscation of allegedly German national–owned property during World War II. While most of these owners were born in Costa Rica and thus in point of fact were German Costa Rican, their ability to retain German citizenship despite birth abroad made them an inviting target during wartime, helping to justify a none-too-generous policy of seizure and nonreturn at the end of the war, usually without compensation. Once those imprisoned in the United States returned to Costa Rica, some would of necessity turn to *beneficio* administration to make ends meet. Early co-op members were at times able to remember, most often with gratitude, the names of the first technicians and plant managers they hired, German Costa Ricans among them. Their loyalty to what remained of the traditional system, not to mention their sense of shared class interests with those who had benefited too often from their own expropriation, would have been reduced after spending months or years in prisoner-of-war camps in Texas.[17]

Still, it seems remarkable that the private processors appear to have done so little to organize a boycott or to threaten technicians thinking of working for the upstart competition—or at least did not achieve these aims. Some sense of the misplaced confidence of the soon-to-be eclipsed processors can be gleaned from the story recounted by Orlando Barquero (figure 4), an early co-op member in Santo Tomás de Santo Domingo de Heredia.[18] As noted previously, the first processing plant that the Libertad co-op managed to purchase was in Santa Rosa, from Amado Sánchez, he of the misplaced confidence about reclaiming the property when the co-op inevitably failed to make its mortgage payments. While the largest processors, the Tournons in Heredia, were not severely threatened in the short run, the smaller *beneficio* owners would face much greater competition for crop supplies once the co-ops came onto the scene. Sánchez and others like him, along with the private processor–dominated coffee industry in Heredia, would soon be only a memory.

At the same time that the coffee co-ops were being formed, a generation of young men was developing a new role in the coffee farm countryside—that of agricultural extension agent. They had earned the equivalent of a high school degree, most often in San José; they knew how to type and to carry out administrative tasks; and they would find themselves offering technical advice and social organization to farmers, even those far removed from the Central Valley. A particularly valuable informant in Tarrazú was José Flores. He was born and returned to work there in 1965 as an eighteen-year-old, after graduating from high school while living with relatives in San José.[19] In addition to his very vivid memories of a long professional career, he had collected hundreds of photographs of his extension activities during the 1960s and 1970s. Several of those images reveal keys to the early reception of improved cultivation techniques as well as the depth of commitment of that pioneer generation of extension agents. The Flores photo archive contains dozens of images of his demonstration exercises showing farmers how to control water flow through rudimentary terracing. Flores was so enamored of the photographic technology that before his supervisor left the region he convinced him to sell him the camera he had used, and preserved it as a family heirloom.

While Flores and the other extension agents were not charged with organizing the co-ops, they clearly were key supporters of their success. Before the co-ops were able to provide on-staff agronomists in the 1970s and 1980s, to advise farmers on cultivation techniques, the extension agents were on the front lines. Perhaps as important in their unofficial support capacity, they organized 4S clubs and youth activities for future farmers. The depth of their commitment to this enterprise, on multiple levels, can be seen in the print literature that Flores also had archived. His extension agent creed (Credo del Extensionista) was no doubt recited many times, but the fact that it was printed on the back page of the monthly magazine of the Inter-American Institute for Cooperation on Agriculture (figure 11), operating in Costa Rica with United States support since 1943, which was full of practical advice for working farmers and their extension agent colleagues, suggests that this was less a liturgical than a practical, ongoing activity.

The diffusion of dwarf seedlings, unlike terracing, began in the Central Valley's oldest, most productive districts, Heredia in particular. There, the co-ops proved to be key transmission belts of innovation, with Tarrazú's

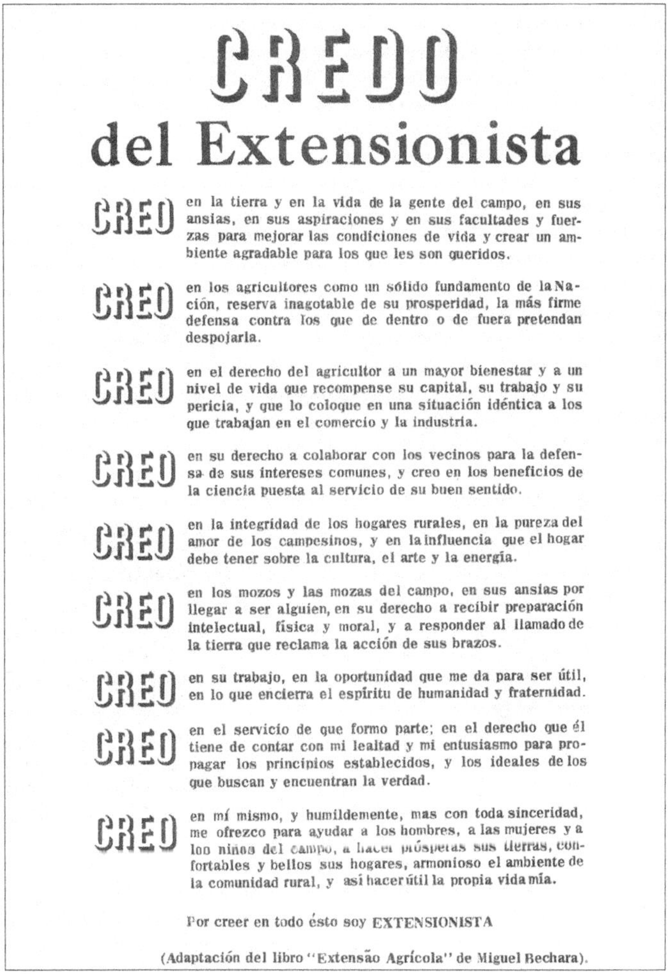

CREDO
del Extensionista

CREO en la tierra y en la vida de la gente del campo, en sus ansias, en sus aspiraciones y en sus facultades y fuerzas para mejorar las condiciones de vida y crear un ambiente agradable para los que les son queridos.

CREO en los agricultores como un sólido fundamento de la Nación, reserva inagotable de su prosperidad, la más firme defensa contra los que de dentro o de fuera pretendan despojarla.

CREO en el derecho del agricultor a un mayor bienestar y a un nivel de vida que recompense su capital, su trabajo y su pericia, y que lo coloque en una situación idéntica a los que trabajan en el comercio y la industria.

CREO en su derecho a colaborar con los vecinos para la defensa de sus intereses comunes, y creo en los beneficios de la ciencia puesta al servicio de su buen sentido.

CREO en la integridad de los hogares rurales, en la pureza del amor de los campesinos, y en la influencia que el hogar debe tener sobre la cultura, el arte y la energía.

CREO en los mozos y las mozas del campo, en sus ansias por llegar a ser alguien, en su derecho a recibir preparación intelectual, física y moral, y a responder al llamado de la tierra que reclama la acción de sus brazos.

CREO en su trabajo, en la oportunidad que me da para ser útil, en lo que encierra el espíritu de humanidad y fraternidad.

CREO en el servicio de que formo parte; en el derecho que él tiene de contar con mi lealtad y mi entusiasmo para propagar los principios establecidos, y los ideales de los que buscan y encuentran la verdad.

CREO en mí mismo, y humildemente, mas con toda sinceridad, me ofrezco para ayudar a los hombres, a las mujeres y a los niños del campo, a hacer prósperas sus tierras, confortables y bellos sus hogares, armonioso el ambiente de la comunidad rural, y así hacer útil la propia vida mía.

Por creer en todo ésto soy EXTENSIONISTA

(Adaptación del libro "Extensão Agrícola" de Miguel Bechara).

FIGURE 11. The Extentionist Creed. (Flores Collection, photo by the author)

co-op sending representatives to study methods being pioneered by farmers and co-ops in Heredia. However, in Heredia itself an institution created in 1948 as a follow-on to the World War II–era cooperative endeavor with the United States, the Inter-American Technical Services in Agricultural Sciences (STICA), played a key, if largely unrecognized, role. One particular informant, Román Rodríguez Argüello, offered a unique perspective on the process. Like other informants, he praised effusively the efforts of a Costa Rican veterinarian/agronomist, Segesimundo "Mundo" Bolaños, who worked in the STICA's technical assistance program in Heredia after his return from training at the Zamorano agricultural school in Honduras.[20]

In 1971, once the dwarf variety bushes had begun to show their promise, Rodríguez entered into a three-way partnership with Bolaños and Carlos Norza, a Costa Rican of Italian descent who headed the STICA program at the time, to rent land near today's international airport for a 130,000-plant coffee seedling operation. As Rodríguez put it, Norza provided the investment capital, Bolaños the know-how, and Rodríguez the strong back, yesterday's version of "sweat equity." While Bolaños worked on this project late in the afternoons (three to six p.m.), after hours from his official, salaried position with STICA in Heredia, it was due entirely to the degree of confidence Rodríguez had in Bolaños's technical abilities, acquired over years in a whole range of non-coffee-related activities, that he decided to risk the enterprise with nothing more than handshakes among friends cum partners.

Three of Rodríguez's siblings had emigrated to the United States in search of work in the 1960s, and ever the small-scale entrepreneur, he partnered with one brother there to purchase used school buses for resale, which Rodríguez drove back through Mexico and Central America. In retirement, he and his wife recently decided to open an Internet café in their village center, in partnership with their son. Clearly, the STICA initiatives Rodríguez and so many other founding-generation co-op members benefited from succeeded precisely because they tapped the myriad resources of a dynamic petty bourgeois class structure capable of seeing and seeking profits, from land rentals and seedlings to Yellowbird school buses driven through police states and civil wars, to the burgeoning demand for Internet access by those not yet able to afford connections in their homes. The public nature of the STICA extension service is as clear, in retrospect, as it succeeded only by leveraging small producers' private initiative, even when the dividing line between official duty and after-hours enterprise may have appeared blurred to outside observers.

Best practices involved everything from terracing to prevent soil erosion to systematic replanting with dwarf variety bushes. However, the combination of bonanza prices owing to the Brazilian frosts of the mid-

1970s and the spectacular productivity increases allowed for by Caturra led at least one informant to discover his own form of best practice: a career change. Roque Mata Naranjo made his way in Costa Rican higher education as a provincial pursuing an agronomy degree. Against all odds, by 1975 he had earned not only his degree but also tenured academic appointments at the University of Costa Rica main campus in San Pedro and at the Universidad Nacional in Heredia.[21]

Mata's renunciation of that pinnacle of achievement and the lifelong salary security must have seemed borderline suicidal to others at the time. Mata recounts that when he applied for the open agricultural extension agent position in his hometown of San Marcos, Tarrazú, in 1975, he was told as much by those filling the post. Even today it defies the imagination, given Costa Ricans' long-standing pattern of rural-to-urban and agricultural-to-professional transitions. However, this was no nostalgia-driven life choice. Recounting his difficult decision, he did not discount his manifest preference for a more rustic, rural way of life or the importance of family ties. But the newly minted academic on the fast track professionally was in a unique position to bring to bear advanced technical knowledge and a deep understanding of Caturra's likely impact on local land tenure and labor patterns. Once again, private initiative to revolutionize coffee farming techniques took place within the co-op framework, not in competition with it.

Unexpected Outcomes: Images and Ironies of Success

Among the many and very striking images and expressions offered by my informants, four will serve to briefly sketch some elements of a profound sense of pride in their achievements, as well as showing how much times have changed, often with painful ironies for themselves.

COYOTES

My colleague in this research enterprise, Wilson Picado, grew up in Tarrazú, and in all our interviews he had to navigate with diplomacy the "insider" and "academic" positions inherent in his local identity and his professional accomplishments. He was the source for one of my earliest arresting moments, when he titled one of his first published essays "*Territorio de coyotes*" ("Land of the Coyotes"). The irony would be apparent only to those familiar with the late twentieth-century slang reference to the traffickers of undocumented laborers to the United States, juxtaposed with the wild animals that are part of frontier farm life. Tarrazú was a "wild" frontier as recently as the 1950s, and yet today it is Costa Rica's premier region for labor migration to New Jersey in search of cash income to save the family farm—perhaps to buy more land, in the best of circumstances—or at the very least to save for a respectable retirement back home. Their place in Tarrazú has been filled by often equally undocumented Nicaraguan and Ngöbe (Indigenous) Panamanian or Costa Rican migrants for the coffee harvests, the local version of the neoliberal and globalized economic system of post-1989 coffee production.[22] Rather than wring their hands over the irony at the center of their families' lives, a smile or laugh accomplishes much more in recognizing how winners and losers are sorted out across borders and reflect Walt Kelly's old saw "We have met the enemy and he is us."

PORTONES

Another image that many times led to shared smiles across the interview table involved the word *portón* (gate), as in both farm gate and entrance to a "gated community." Marco Tulio Zamora gave clearest voice to the outrage against the old system of arbitrary landlord power when he denounced his own relatives' control of the public roads that passed through their property by simply closing the fence gate. Many examples of this old-style gate at the entrance of a working farm in Heredia can still be seen in Heredia, but many more gates guard the entrance to recently built residential zones (figure 12).

However, several other informants had greater interest in discussing much more recent events than those of the 1950s that Zamora privileged. They reflected, at times bitterly, on the conversion of much of the best coffee lands, including their own, into condominiums in the novel, late-1990s Costa Rican phenomenon of gated communities with their own version of the *portón* restricting access. Some worried about how this very lucrative process was destroying the co-op's ability to employ its installed capacity to process only its own members' crop, but others were only too happy to cash in via urbanization and sale of lots. Nearly all those who had sold lots reserved some of their most critical comments for the municipal governments who (in 2009) were severely slowing down the process by

FIGURE 12. Entrance to a gated community in San Pablo de Heredia. (Photo by the author)

withholding water connection permits for new construction, out of fear of further burdening already compromised acquifers.[23]

ADULT DAY CARE

The only female founding-generation interviewee lived in San Isidro de Heredia. Anita Azofeifa Zamora (figure 13) offered a story full of twists and turns that stretched the imagination even when retold years later.[24] She and her husband, Héctor Ramírez Cháves, began producing coffee on a tiny farm in the early 1950s. Her father had been a founding member of La Libertad co-op, and she would eventually join, but only after the premature death of her husband left her to raise their ten children alone. She continued to produce some coffee with her older children's help, but she also overcame a great deal of gender prejudice to become the first woman employed as a salesperson in the local co-op's basic grains and provisions warehouse (the *estanco* of the Consejo Nacional de Producción). In 2009, seventy-five years old and retired herself, she coordinated excursions and activities for older adults in her home town.

Azofeifa's goals in life, however, had little to do with any of this. Her greatest personal regret and disappointment was not being able to study beyond grade school, so she took great pride in having kept her children

FIGURE 13. Doña Anita Azofeifa Zamora in her living room in San Isidro. (Photo by the author)

in school far beyond her own grade level. In fact, several earned college degrees with the help of scholarships, but only after their mother had managed to marshal her earnings from coffee and selling the production of her milk cows to keep them in high school down the mountain, in Santo Domingo.

Azofeifa is painfully aware that the coffee lands that were once hers are being converted to house lots, including the land she has already divided among her children. With an air of both accomplishment and resignation, she told me, "The coffee's about done . . . All that's left is to put up the [last] for sale sign, so that they all [her ten children] have a plot, while I'm alive. I wanted to sell so that there would be no problems, so they all would know I had done my part."

After the recorder was turned off, our conversation continued for a few minutes, about the upcoming co-op assembly and whether we might see each other there again. Reflecting on how her own situation was far from unique, she quipped that the assemblies are "just like my elder care outings." When I boarded the local bus for Santa Bárbara de Heredia on the Saturday morning of the annual assembly, I was pleasantly surprised to greet and chat with Guido Rojas, another informant I had interviewed previously. His own version of Azofeifa's quip was to lament the fact that I would not find a single "face under fifty" once we arrived at the assembly. While both informants were fairly accurate as to age distributions, it was no less true that Azofeifa, and elderly widows like her, were not the only women members in attendance.[25]

AN ENTIRE SOCIAL ORDER PAST

A recurring theme of nearly all the interviews was the rubbing up against each other of memories of great success amid even greater transformations during a single lifetime. One of my most extensive interviews was with a former colleague and fellow foreign-born faculty member at the Universidad Nacional, the Chilean sociologist José Cazanga, author of one of the most detailed studies of coffee co-ops at the height of their power and influence in the late 1970s and early 1980s.[26] While most of our conversation drifted toward an understanding of how and when neoliberal orthodoxies of the 1980s had taken hold in the Costa Rican countryside, we could hardly avoid reminiscing about the days when those very same children of Anita Azofeifa, Guido Rojas, Orlando Barquero, and so very many other coffee farmers had been our ambitious, first-generation college students. Indeed, even then, few had any intention of returning to the farm if they could avoid it, but the passing of that very brief moment in time was itself based on such a curious combination of success and transformation.

We somewhat sheepishly recalled just how easy it had been for us, even as green card–carrying, legally employed foreigners, to gain university employment as enrollments exploded. We recalled that the tiniest of agricultural producers seemed newly able to acquire cheap pickups on credit in the late 1970s, only to then ruefully admit that, as beginning assistant professors, even we could. For that decade, at least, the logic appeared to be one of a coherent social democratic model championed by the PLN. Neither of us recognized all that much that was familiarly "rural" from our Chilean or U.S. backgrounds. But we did sense that the entire model hinged on the social organization and transformation of the coffee sector. Cazanga knew it because he studied it in depth, and I knew it simply through living in its heartland for much of the decade.

From his detailed knowledge of more than a dozen coffee co-ops, Cazanga was struck particularly by many of the tendencies noted here. The weight of the middling to larger producers within the co-ops was visible from the start, including one case in which, Cazanga estimated, perhaps a third of the co-op's coffee was produced by a single member. The technical know-how of the average coffee farmer, as well as their semi-urbanized environment, was something for which his Chilean experiences had not prepared him. Detailed knowledge of the workings of the processing plants allowed their newly acquired *beneficios* to succeed, and this same "quick study" talent allowed them to aggressively educate themselves about marketing, about hiring "brokers" for the export trade from early on, and about the benefits of dwarf varieties for which they themselves produced seedlings during the 1970s.

Well before the rise to hegemony of neoliberal paradigms, the capital accumulated by co-op members during the coffee boom and transformation made its way into not only house lot sales but also light industry of all kinds. Cazanga pointed to a particularly telling example of this as our conversation came to an end. Back in the late 1970s, when we were buying our first vehicles, whether sedans or pickups, they were stripped-down, locally assembled versions of Japanese and Korean makes. By the late 1980s, small-scale coffee producer profits had found their way to the ownership of the Honda import dealership, a veritable icon of the new order. It had never been downsized and cheapened for local assembly, and it quickly became the auto of choice among neoliberalism's rapidly expanding professional classes, not infrequently the children of co-op coffee farmers.

The educational and social mobility of this new generation created a new lived experience in which virtually none of the same work routines, technical know-how, organizational needs, or ideological commitments would live on beyond a rapidly aging coffee co-op farmer population. Success was everywhere to be seen, but it came at a very steep price indeed for the cooperative-era social democratic model itself. However, the golden bean and global trade also experienced their own radical turn-of-the-century transformation, which we turn to in chapter 4. The pathway from the humorous and lovable Juan Valdez to the quality competitions, no longer disputed by the co-ops but by the microprocessors of the gourmet world, points us in the same direction: to the rise of a new world order and the disappearance of a whole social order past.

4

From Co-op Reformism to Gourmet Globalization

Java Joe, Juan Valdez, Starbucks, and Café Britt

For today's coffee producers and consumers, heirs to more than three decades of globalization and its reconfiguration of commodity chain networks, nothing is more obvious than that its price depends directly on its "quality." Commonplace, common sense; many times an argument persuades merely by its affirmation. But the word "quality" itself turns out to be somewhat subjective, opaque, and even mysterious. Worse yet, it is wrong to use it in singular form, since what distinguishes the era of globalization is in fact the seemingly infinite proliferation of qualities and prices, which are much more abundant and visible than in earlier eras. Some preachers of the benefits of the new order and its abundant choices eagerly contribute to the process of social amnesia. Surrendering themselves fully to contemporary rejoicing over the new freedoms—to choose and to simultaneously define oneself socially within the mass of consumers—helps erase from memory the antecedents of differentiation and the discourses about "quality" within the global coffee trade.

This chapter offers two types of evidence and arguments. First, we will explore the empirical evidence of the co-op movement's success in disputing the predominance of private processors during the period of the International Coffee Agreement (ICA), basically from the mid-1960s to the early 1990s. Immediately thereafter, the national and international private firms retook the initiative and constructed a new trading system after the collapse of the last ICA, in 1989. Second, the bulk of the text will present an analysis of the evolution of systems of and discourses about "quality," which predates its rediscovery at the end of the twentieth century and its overwhelming triumph in our day.

Complex, indeed, are the visible and foreseeable consequences of the new regime of privately establishing radically differential prices, particularly when practices and institutions are no longer based on cooperation to regulate and limit competition but on rewards and platforms to foment it. This regime deserves precisely the kind of prophetic analysis offered fully two decades ago by William Roseberry, who looked at "yuppie coffees" and their consumers at the start of a single sociological process, whether we call it globalization, gentrification, or new forms of social class identity in the postmodern and postindustrial era. For this analysis, our resources and allies will be the works of dearly departed colleagues like Roseberry and Michael Jiménez as well as figures more mythical than real, such as Juan Valdez.[1] For some contemporary readers, figures like Juan Valdez and his dear mule Conchita may seen somewhere between folkloric and pathetic, but the history of their publicity campaigns, just as the ICA was about to collapse, offers revealing clues as to the deep origins of the triumphal discourses of quality and social distinction in the era of Starbucks and Café Britt.

Reform and Competition: Origins and Achievements of Coffee Co-op Processing

The initial success, or failure, of the co-op movement depended almost completely on the co-ops' ability to acquire processing plants and to compete with private processors by attracting members through better prices and conditions. As we saw in chapter 2, the co-ops enjoyed spectacular success during the first two or three decades of their existence, not only wresting from their private competitors control of the bulk of the rapidly expanding national harvest but also forcing greater price competition and flexibility, to the benefit of all coffee farmers, whether they were co-op members or not. In Heredia, this was particularly evident in reference to the triad of major private processors (Tournon, Rohrmoser, and Montealegre), but it was no less true in Tarrazú.

The rise and consolidation of the co-op processing plants was spectacular at both the national and the local levels. In graphs 1 and 2, we saw that after less than two decades the co-ops were managing to process one-third or more of the national harvest—and to exceed the volume of the private processors in Heredia. Such results were possible owing to the broad popularity of the co-op option with coffee growers of all sizes and to the support of some of the wealthiest. The five Santo Domingo and San Isidro clans identified in chapter 2 (Barquero, Chacón, Rodríguez, Villalobos, and Zamora) made up a large part of the nucleus of La Libertad. Likewise, the Chilean–Costa Rican author of the classic study of the rise of the co-ops in the 1970s, José Cazanga, estimated that up to a third of the harvest processed by an Alajuela co-op was delivered by a single member. Eventually, this same pattern came to characterize the co-ops in the southern part of the country, the fastest growing from the 1980s forward, from Tarrazú and Dota to the Valle de El General, all the way to San Vito and Sabalito along the frontier with Panama.[2] Nonetheless, the initial co-op success in the 1960s and 1970s took place in the Central Valley, still the dominant production zone and soon to witness its own version of a productive revolution, perhaps not typically "green," but anything but "red."

The recovery of the private processors was not long delayed, however. From the 1990s on, they gained market share and eclipsed the co-op dominance, clearly exceeding the latter's role today. Nevertheless, the role of the seventeen coffee co-ops remains strong today, since they processed 36.5% of the national harvest in 2010–2011 and 41.5% in 2014–2015, even when the epicenter of co-op production has moved to the south.[3] The truly new phenomenon of the past decade or more is the growth of so-called *microbeneficios,* which in many cases are owned by former members of the same co-ops that are no longer receiving their harvest. These micro processing plants accounted for 34.5% of processing in 2014–2015.[4] In fact, the *microbeneficios* follow the same logic as the equally novel phenomenon within the gourmet market, the annual quality competitions or prizes. Although it is true that La Libertad increased its own volume somewhat after the failure of Santa Rosa and San Juanillo in the early 1990s, the local experience in Heredia reaffirmed once again the national trend: the recovery of private processors' dominant role.

The generalized urbanization of the Central Valley, particularly in San José and Heredia, has led to a reduction in the area in coffee and its harvest, up to 20% by some estimates, accelerating its replacement in the national scheme by the previously peripheral zones in the south (Tarrazú and, above all, San Isidro de El General and Coto Brus) and in western Alajuela (Naranjo), the areas that today compete for the prize for best-quality coffee nationally. The five southern co-ops (Tarrazú, Dota, El

General, San Vito, and Sabalito) saw their percentage of national harvest processed grow from 4.3% to 20.6% between 1964–1965 and 2002–2003. The same process of expansion characterized the private sector in the south as well. The percentage change in Heredia's co-ops in the national harvest went in the opposite direction, increasing at the height of the conversion to Caturra in the 1970s, from 1.5% in 1964–1965 to 5% in 1980–1981, falling thereafter to 2.9% in 2002–2003.[5]

The Discreet Charm of "Good Taste" Renewed in the Postindustrial World: Antecedents and Innovations in the World of Coffee

During its golden age in the second half of the twentieth century, co-op reformism managed to capture a greater proportion of profits in its international commodity chain. It did this by eliminating bottlenecks and monopolies, acquiring processing and marketing capacities for its members within an international system that regulated and limited competition among producers while avoiding much of the discourse about quality differentiation. Beyond the most basic differences (such as *robusta* versus *arábigo*, highland grown or not, shaded or full sun, handpicked or mechanically harvested, the grade of dried beans, and wet or dry processing), quality discourse had less visible impact on the setting of prices and the marketing strategies used by growers, roasters, and merchants under the ICA from 1942 to 1989. Pricing and marketing were always present, yes, but both Colombian growers and the U.S. roaster and merchandiser Folgers mainly appealed to the vague notion and slogan of "mountain grown," using altitude as a guarantee of quality to justify its slightly higher prices or instill brand loyalty. But the weak presence of a discourse about quality in the midcentury world of coffee has a complicated history that needs to be understood before attempting an analysis of the massive expansion of its weight and visibility in the postindustrial social world.

Three decades ago, Michael Jiménez invited us to have coffee with quintessential North Americans of the Fordist era, who invented the "coffee break" as a social ritual of the industrial routine. Even when coffee demand worldwide depended on fomenting the habit of consuming it at home, the U.S. public spaces of that time stood out as quasi industrial.

These were not the small shops specialized in serving coffee that were typical of other nations at the time—and of the entire world in our own era. No other nation is so identified with prize competition spectacles—from dance to the point of collapsing from exhaustion, in the midst of the Depression of the 1930s, to massive consumption of food or drink—as a symbol, between idolatrous and absurd, of pride in its material plenty. Jiménez recounted how one Gus Comstock was the winner of a local competition in Fergus Falls, Minnesota, in January 1927, surviving without visible harm the ingestion of eighty cups of coffee in the space of 7 hours and 15 minutes.[6] In our own time, every year we are offered the "sporting" spectacle of a hot dog eating contest, which crowns champions like Joey Chestnut, whose belly found room for seventy-one hot dogs, buns included, in ten minutes during the Nathan's Famous competition, held on July 4, 2019.[7] It goes without saying that in all these performances, from the everyday to the circus-like, there was no hint of any clear idea of the "quality" or prestige of the product itself.

In the everyday marketing of coffee, the goal was to habituate the consumer, privileging above all taste, which was attributed more to the toaster's formula than to the origin or quality of the bean itself. This was achieved by emotively associating coffee consumption with spaces for socializing, created by the technology of its mass production and consumption. The longed-for rest the coffee break offered, the friendship with relatives and friends drinking and eating out together, waited on by familiar faces cum friends, too—both scenarios offered attractions that depended less on the taste of the coffee sipped, hot or lukewarm, than on the conversation that accompanied it. From the enormous percolators in the first half of the century, electric appliances capable of straining several liters of coffee at once, to the ubiquitous vending machines for instant coffee in offices and schools in the 1970s, it would be hard to find even the most minimum discourses about or choices based on the quality of the raw material itself. Tasters and savorers these coffee drinkers were not, although later their children and grandchildren would identify and distinguish themselves as such, with comparable symbols and self-images.

As early as the 1920s and 1930s, U.S. trade organizations (importers, roasters, and merchandisers) recognized not only that international agreements would suit them, assuring stable prices, but also that rewarding the "taste" of the end product (repeatable ad infinitum) and the context of its preparation over the quality (and of course the price) of the original beans would serve them as well. As Jiménez showed, the trade association members understood perfectly how they controlled that part of the process, while the foreign growers and their trade representatives fought to validate their discourse on quality and the prices based on it. The U.S. market was, in effect, the only one in which the major importers and merchants followed this strategic commercial practice: blending beans of different quality (a minority of more expensive, highland-grown, hand-picked Colombian or Central American beans combined with a majority of cheaper Brazilian beans), betting that taste mattered more to their clients than origin brands or intrinsic quality of the beans. Of course, the underlying logic of the wager assumed the oligopolistic control they exercised over the U.S. market at the time.

The deindustrialization of the 1970s and 1980s led not only to a radical reduction in the proportion of wage workers in industry and unions but also to a contraction of factory spaces for the daily routines of collective coffee consumption. Almost simultaneously, new commercial spaces for individual consumption were recreated, the coffeehouse chains (Starbucks is the iconic but not the only case), in place of cafeterias under the same Fordist factory or administrative office roof. But the renewed charm of "good taste" was not born from the lucid, prophetic minds of the marketers of supposedly high-quality coffee alone. The recognition that the quality factor existed was always latent, and others within and, above all, outside the United States saw in coffee and its consumption other possible motives, meanings, and practices. Before returning to the recent history of the triumph of gourmet coffees, then, we will try to follow the trail of different sites and expressions of the coffee quality consciousness that would have such an impact in our day.

The history of coffee consumption in the United States—from its rise in the nineteenth century after the break with Great Britain and its teas from India, whose high taxes helped to provoke that break, to the era of Fordist industrialization, and even today—has been characterized by only faint echoes of the discourse on quality, coming from the least expected corners. Examples abound, but we begin with an impish one, extracted from the birth of large-scale trade, and another, rather more pathetic instance, from our gourmet era.

While researching the early history of Guatemalan coffee exports to California, David McCreery encountered a Guatemalan trader too smart for his own good, who shipped his product not to San Francisco but to Indonesia in order to disguise and reship it as if it were a product of Java, as the archipelago was called at that time. He failed in his plan to fool the buyers in San Francisco when he was discovered, but he offers us a tremendous example of the powerful incentive for associating oneself with a rival product considered of better quality in the mid-nineteenth century.[8] Moreover, the word "java" has remained in the jargon of U.S. consumers for a century and a half, from the reference to "a cup of java," to G.I. Joe in World War II and his nickname Java Joe, to Starbucks's popular Java Chip Frappuccino.

The other, more pathetic example comes from the hamburger chain McDonald's. For years now, its advertising slogan has highlighted the supposed quality of its coffee by saying that it is "100% *arábigo.*" In fact, practically 100% of coffee sold in the United States is also 100% *arábigo*, (that is, not *robusta*), but ignoring this reality seems to be the point of departure for such an advertising campaign, which paradoxically exploits both the consumer's ignorance and their desire for distinction, based on a quality criterion somewhere between meaningless and irrelevant.[9]

The most successful coffee "brand" or advertising image in all of U.S. history prior to our gourmet era was, without a doubt Juan Valdez, a character invented and patented in 1959 by the 300,000 (today more than 500,000) growers joined in the National Federation of Coffee Growers of Colombia, with the help of the publicity firm Doyle Dane Bernbach of New York's Madison Avenue, the firm responsible for the successful advertising campaign for Volkswagen when it fully entered the U.S. market in the 1960s. During its first decade, Juan Valdez was played by a Cuban actor, José Duval. Later, Antioqueño Carlos Sánchez was selected, and until 2006 he was the affable and mustachioed Colombian farmer, with his poncho over the shoulder and his mule Conchita at his side. His success in convincing different publics of the advantages of consuming Colombian coffee was extraordinary.[10]

The degree of recognition and acceptance of Juan Valdez by the North American public is nearly mythical in the advertising industry. By the end of the 1980s, just before the collapse of the ICA system, several market studies showed that up to 83% of U.S. adults recognized his iconic image as the Colombian coffee brand, compared with barely 4% at the beginning of the 1960s. Even more impressive, 53% of informants were able to recall his name as well. The impact of three decades of Colombian coffee advertising campaigns was very noteworthy. Even without Juan Valdez, in silhouette or image, or any words, large majorities of consumers recognized the tiny "100% Colombian" emblem that each package always carried, a simple line drawing suggesting mountain peaks. The connection with the earlier slogan of "Mountain grown" was surely no coincidence, nor was the campaign's nostalgic attempt to evoke empathy for this folkloric "common man" who supposedly harvested his own fruit by hand (the other "advantage" or source of "quality") in that mythic and mountainous Colombia of rustic, cobblestone streets, with no form of transportation other than the beast of burden.

True enough, the first advertising images of Juan Valdez for the U.S. market openly employed some of the most traditional and condescending Anglo-Saxon stereotypes about Latin Americans, who were supposedly isolated from the modern, commercial world, whether they were pictured as fearsome and bloody primitives or, as in this case, what Costa Ricans know as the benevolent but naive figure of the *concho,* or rustic, timid backwoodsman. Nevertheless, the federation (more than the advertising firm, one supposes) managed to plant other, more positive messages within the images, such as about the superiority of highland coffee and the tenacity of growers tending personally to their groves and harvesting by hand with that same owner's care.

However, what interests us here is not the stereotypes about Latin Americans but rather their hidden opposite, that is, how it was that the advertising campaigns, at the height of Juan Valdez's influence as icon in the 1980s, reflected a deep knowledge of North America's mentality, including such stereotypes. The campaigns stimulated sales not by appealing to condescending empathy or quality criteria but with a humor that was at times ersatz and other times kitsch but always socially leveling, from vulgar or picaresque to faddish or affected. At the same time, the campaigns destined for the European market depended just as much on humor but always pointed to the simultaneous reverence for social distinction and the supposed quality of the product—precisely what would come to characterize the U.S. market with the rise of the gourmet era.

Some of the images used in the various Juan Valdez advertising campaigns in North America, Europe, and Latin America at the end of the 1980s and in the early 1990s reveal clearly the different mentalities that are being probed.[11] Two images targeting the North American market that compare Colombian coffee and its icon with popular media phenomena employ fairly simple humor while remaining current. In one, as pair figure skaters, Juan Valdez holds Conchita above his head as they fly across the ice (referring to the newly popular iced coffee). An even more "inside joke" on novel fads of the time employs the silhouette of Juan and Conchita inside their own office for consultation and sales of aromatherapy products.

Another humorous trope for the U.S. market ventured into sexual terrain, either picaresque or trendy, depending on the image and its message. The imagery used ranged from subtle satire for both the U.S. and European/Latin American markets to a much more direct play on words from U.S. popular culture of the time. The subtle message was expressed by a classic pair of statues covered only with fig leaves, where the woman resists the seductive offer of her male companion, saying, "Very tempting, but I'm saving myself for Colombian coffee." In a trendy example typical of the U.S. market, one ad portrayed Juan Valdez and Conchita as surfers, with a macho motto of the moment: "Grab life by the beans." These images, with their humor, social commentary, and borderline vulgarity, were ad tested before being launched in the U.S. market. Clearly, they were entertaining rather than offending their viewers.

The images chosen for the European and Latin American campaigns, in contrast, employed messages affirming the high quality of the product and the elevated social position of those who consumed such products and services. This message is spelled out explicitly in a U.S. ad with the image of Juan and Conchita embodied on a milk cow, producer of the liquid worthy of accompanying Colombian coffee. In the Latin American and European markets, the caption was simply "*La crème de la crème.*" In other images (employed in international airlines' onboard magazines of the time), we see a woman ascending in a chairlift at a ski resort, receiving a cup of coffee from a hand floating in the air, with the motto "100% uplifting." The suggestion of the woman's privileged status, with the hand of an anonymous servant offering her the cup of coffee, could hardly be more obvious to the prospective European consumers of Colombian coffee.

Yet another image for the European and Latin American markets combined the message of high social status, high-quality coffee, and air travel by using birds flying in a V formation to outline the image of Juan and Conchita, inviting viewers to "Fly first class." The intent was not to motivate the traveler to change cabins, paying more for a first-class ticket; rather, the point was to insinuate an equivalence between the quality of Colombian coffee and the presumed (and now achieved) status of these same airborne readers. Reflecting the relation between socioeconomic status and degree of access to air travel, which was far more available to the masses in the United States, the message in effect congratulated those who traveled by plane and thus ratified their superior status (whether real or imagined, for advertisers it is all the same), which was confirmed once again with a cup of unsurpassable Colombian coffee at an altitude of 10,000 meters.

Another ad reveals even more about the different transatlantic mentalities examined at the end of the ICA and the beginning of the gourmet era. It synthesizes remarkably the contrast between messages directed to distinct markets, with the United States leveling downward and the European and Latin American affirming and reflecting more elitist values of quality ("100% uplifting"). Proudly announcing the arrival of Colombian coffee to its North American flights in 1985, American Airlines placed our fast friends Juan Valdez and Conchita in passenger seats next to each other, provoking the typical, universal reaction of amusement in the child, the elder, the aristocrat, and the commoner equally.

In the three decades since Juan Valdez and Conchita boarded American Airlines, however, the United States has undergone a profound transformation, with very rapid urbanization and greatly increased income inequality. In effect, its coffee consumers in the gourmet era have gone from provincials to Parisians in a single generation. Perhaps the most prescient of all the Juan Valdez advertisement images was one that anticipated, while commenting on, our shared "Europeanization" and the brand loyalty of the recent past. The humorous rendering of Colombian coffee beans as if they were grapes, highlighting their trademark status in French ("Appellation Colombie Contrôlée"), not only made the quality and price comparison to fine wines directly but also foreshadowed perhaps the single most contentious issue for coffee producers in the gourmet era, the struggle to trademark and control place-name origins in coffee marketing. From a lowest common denominator humor in its early forays in the

U.S. market to a "100% uplifting" defense of quality discourses even before they became dominant in the gourmet era, Juan Valdez and Colombian coffee proved to be symbols and products as elastic as they were effective.

Costa Rica Before the Co-ops: The Photography of Manuel Gómez Miralles

Before we expand upon the significance of the ad campaigns, let us touch upon the visual recording of an earlier era before the co-ops. Before small and middling farmers joined together to form cooperatives, the wealthiest growers with processing plants and export connections called the tune. Perhaps the best chronicler of that period was the photographer Manuel Gómez Miralles in his *Album Costa Rica, América Central,* first published in 1922, many of whose images were later sold as picture postcards (see, for example, figures 14–19). His images depict various facets of the coffee industry, from cultivation to harvesting, processing, and transport, providing a gendered visual record attentive to both social spaces and enterprise scale.

FIGURE 14. Harvesting coffee: Family labor awaiting their piece-rate wages. Archivo Nacional de Costa Rica, Photographic Collection, CR-AN-AH-FO-219882.

FIGURE 15. From farm to processing plant: Oxcarts hauling harvested coffee. Archivo Nacional de Costa Rica, Photographic Collection, CR-AN-AH-FO-002188.

FIGURE 16. Male spaces: Processing-plant workers drying coffee. Archivo Nacional de Costa Rica, Photographic Collection, CR-AN-AH-FO-002189.

FIGURE 17. Male spaces: Gang field labor on large farms. Archivo Nacional de Costa Rica, Photographic Collection, CR-AN-AH-FO-002187.

FIGURE 18. Female spaces: Grading processed coffee beans for export. Archivo Nacional de Costa Rica, Photographic Collection, CR-AN-AH-FO-002244.

FIGURE 19. From Costa Rica to the world: Oxcarts hauling processed and bagged coffee to the railhead. Archivo Nacional de Costa Rica, Photographic Collection, CR-AN-AH-FO-002191.

Yuppie Coffees, Co-ops, and Competition: The Rise of the Gourmet Market

The ad campaign images of Juan Valdez discussed above juxtapose mentalities and coffee markets as they existed at the end of the 1980s and the ICA era. But these ads invite a second reading, to view how far we have come since then in terms of marketing in the United States. Today, any ad image for Starbucks or its competitors tends to employ messages that establish a visible "gap" between one's own items of consumption and those preferred by the commoner masses, an approach so necessary for turn-of-the-century mall shoppers anywhere in the world. (The Gap casual clothing chain was born during the same transitional era.) As with practically all areas of social life, from residence and marriage patterns to the most daily consumer habits, the Europeanization of U.S. society, at least on the two coasts and in the largest urban centers, has been the constant recipe.

Call it globalization, gentrification, "yuppification," or simply the dizzying growth of socioeconomic inequality.[12]

The change did not come suddenly, nor was it a simple consequence of the collapse of the ICA in 1989. It had deep roots in the previous two decades. The ever more marked tendency toward the differentiation of niche and segmented markets, toward middle- and high-income consumers, required several innovations. The containerization revolution in maritime and land transport of commodities, with substantial reductions in the cost of moving both finished products and raw materials and component parts, was generalized more than ever with the Asian manufacturing boom of the 1960s. Likewise, it required the development of much more sophisticated models of geographic analysis, before Global Positioning Systems. In the United States, at least, it meant the capacity to carry out much more fine-grained analyses of per capita and household incomes, no longer employing the old rail and highway systems but rather postal zip codes as georeferents, linked to data from the census and the Commerce, Treasury, and Labor departments. Any investor of average intelligence could determine where best to locate and build a new mall, but not just anyone would be able to foresee and execute a business expansion project of up to five hundred small shops or coffeehouses in barely a couple of years.

Paradoxically, the success of the Fordist model in providing enormous quantities of consumer goods at low prices became its Achilles' heel, once the wealthiest consumers tired of the monotony and lack of distinction and began to massively demand something different. The ironies of the transition process are innumerable, but one in particular will suffice as an example here. In the 1960s and 1970s, cheap blue jeans, basic and patched over and over again, practically functioned as the flag of a generation in rebellion against consumer society. Less than two decades later, those same jeans had migrated to the most expensive and exclusive shops and shelves, now not only for youth but for any consumer searching for quality and distinction. And even though they were more expensive, those jeans were ripped or patched, stone prewashed so that they would appear more "comfortable" or "valued" as (visibly) "used" (although new).

Coffee also entered the new commercial scene, thanks both to the Brazilian frosts of the mid-1970s and to the efforts of coffee merchants to counter the already notable decline in per capita coffee consumption in the United States. The frosts after 1975 had a major impact on coffee's international price, ushering in the golden years for Costa Rican coffee. In the United States, there were even congressional investigations into possible price manipulation in the market, without major impacts, of course. Beginning in the major coastal cities, however, small importers and roasters took advantage of the rise in prices of the raw ingredient to try out another market strategy: if the regular or poor quality coffee available cost twice as much as before, perhaps the time had come to offer indignant consumers a higher-quality product for a few cents more than that, since they would have to pay more for their coffee regardless. At first, distribution was local or regional, especially in small shops or high-end delis, emphasizing higher quality and with varietals identified by origin, as being from Brazil or Colombia, for example, and not simply as *arábigo* or *robusta*. The opening of coffeehouse chains was still far off, but Starbucks was born precisely from one of these local experiences, in Seattle, Washington.

The institutional proponents of coffee consumption in the United States, coffee executives and their advertisers, recognized two challenges in the early 1980s. On the one hand, per capita consumption had declined since the 1960s. In 1962, 74.7% of the U.S. adult population drank coffee, while in 1988 only 50% did. Worse yet, among those who drank coffee, the number of daily cups had gone from 3.12 in 1962, to 2.02 in 1980, to 1.67 in 1988. On the other hand, they suspected that the decrease was owing not so much to new health concerns as to the loss of the youth generation, which preferred soft drinks. A dark panorama and tremendous challenge.

The response came quickly and was brilliantly embedded in the process of social class reconfiguration during the postmodern and postindustrial era. In a speech to the Green Coffee Association of New York in 1981, Kenneth Roman Jr., an adman for Maxwell House, argued for a new strategy directed at different segments of the consumer market, with at least five categories—or in today's jargon, demographics. He even assigned fictitious names to each group: the Grays (a thirtysomething, demanding, high-income married couple); the Pritchetts (a fiftyish married couple, retired and low income); Karen Sperling (a thirtysomething, single working woman with little time to make coffee); the Taylors (a sixtyish married couple with health concerns about coffee consumption); and Joel (a young college student with whom the challenge was assumed to be the soft drink competition). In fact, the new and growing gourmet market in the United States was born thanks to the resounding success in capturing the first and last groups of this fictional 1981 story in the real world of the 1990s and later.

Roman and his colleagues would soon know the relevant statistics. While per capita consumption declined, the specialty coffee sector (our "gourmet" category) within overall imports increased very rapidly, between 30% and 50% per year during the 1980s, from some 14 million pounds in 1980 to 40 million pounds in 1983. The specialty market was worth $330 million in 1985, $420 million in 1986, and $500 million in 1987, when it represented 8% of all imported coffee in the United States. The phenomenon took place behind the back of the dominant large firms, which were very late to recognize the emergent market for "good taste," as opposed to the market based on reliable uniformity and "taste" in the sense of habituation to a roaster's formula. In the early 1980s, there were fewer than two hundred roasting firms in the United States, and the four largest controlled 75% of the national market. Today, more than three decades later, the traditional or "historic" coffee brands have lost the great majority of the market to Starbucks and its imitators born under the gourmet label, not only on the shelves of shops selling "fine coffees" but also on the shelves of the everyday national supermarket chains.

Although gourmet coffee no doubt offered a quality that was superior to the traditional product, problems and contradictory strategies soon appeared. The product was first sold in the more selective and expensive shops, or in the poorest co-ops, and the consumer was tempted by the sale of beans in traditional nineteenth-century burlap sacks, by the illusion of some connection with the site of production, or by the "selectivity" of small quantities. But disappointment was just around the corner when, woken from the dream, the buyer realized that of course none of it was real.

Nevertheless, Starbucks and its clones have used the same tactic and image, placing the sacks in plain sight and labeling coffee with the names of supposedly historically coffee-based regions or farms, without any proof of origin of the beans themselves. Worse yet, they have employed the tactic of confusing origin with "blend" or "style." A coffee is no longer "from" Kenya, Sumatra, or Blue Mountain, Jamaica; it is Kenya Blend or Sumatra Style, for instance. Or they focus on "flavor," shamelessly imitating their historic enemy, the oligopolistic roasters they had replaced, seeking to consolidate the loyalty of consumers whose geographic or varietal powers of discernment remain as minimal as they are lamentable.

The strategy to win over the "Joel" generation was undoubtedly the most important, for obvious reasons of future markets, and was the most successful. For young people in the United States in the 1990s and thereafter, malls and coffee shops replaced many other sites and practices as "public spaces" to get together. Some even believe that their renewed, massive coffee consumption in public places of entertainment diminished somewhat the furtive consumption of alcohol as obligatory companion of social encounters in previous decades. The invitation to the Joels to begin developing a loyalty to coffee took maximum advantage of this emphasis on "taste," not only when roasting but also with the practice of adding aerosols, essences, or flavors to the roasted beans themselves; of selling syrups to add to the drink; or of developing many types of iced coffees mixed with other ingredients. The quality of the coffee bean, traditionally understood, figured little in the young consumer's calculus of a recipe with shots of syrup added, or with more chocolate and cream than coffee.

What the strategies of all the coffeehouse chains had in common was their precise location, which long ago passed the saturation point. Every university district worthy of consideration had two or three per neighborhood, following not only the logic of capturing the Joels but also established practice, since the investment in the first market trials of the gourmet market were also located in such districts. The areas of greatest population density and highest incomes reveal a saturation barely imaginable two or three decades ago. In the center of Manhattan, in an area of no more than 70 hectares, dominated by skyscrapers and the hotel industry, can be found no fewer than twenty-five Starbucks—without counting the outlets inside the same hotels and in bookshops authorized to sell the product, at times with two or three visible from across the street.

Ironically, while the gourmet sector arose due to the Fordist excesses of its predecessors, their alienating uniformity and scale, its own success rests in large part on similar post-Fordist (although neo-Fordist) practices, replicating innumerable outlets themselves. Starbucks does not sell franchises, the common practice of most popular hotel and restaurant chains since the 1960s. Its new challenge is to continue convincing its consumers that choosing and remaining loyal to it confirms their "good taste," even as they enter in their preferred brand's shop no. 1,000 to enjoy a cup of coffee that may not be from Kenya but does *taste* like Kenya flavor.

We have used the Starbucks example so often not just for its iconic value within the process but also because it is estimated that at the start of the twenty-first century, the firm became the largest buyer of Costa Rican coffee. The giant of the sector worldwide, Starbucks was born in Seattle in 1971. By mid-2016 it was present in seventy-two countries, with more than 23,000 shops, at least 13,000 of them in the United States. Its weight as a buyer in Costa Rica began to be felt at the end of the past century, and in 2014 it acquired a coffee farm of some 240 hectares as an experimental station, which has already produced at least five new varietals in joint trials with the Instituto del Café de Costa Rica (ICAFE), responding to the challenges of coffee rust (*roya del café*) as well as climate change and decreasing rainfall in the traditional coffee zones.

In Costa Rica, Starbucks's pioneer counterpart as leader of the gourmet market was undoubtedly Café Britt. Beginning in 1985, Café Britt pointed out the path to follow, combining the tourism boom (offering tours of its coffee *beneficio* in Heredia) with sales of its own brand, first within the country and then abroad. It opened its first kiosk in the Juan Santamaría International Airport in 2001 and today has a presence in ten countries, with 140 shops and around one thousand employees.

Consumers' recognition of the iconic images of these firms in each country surely equals or exceeds Juan Valdez's documented recognition in the U.S. market around 1990. The private processors quickly imitated Café Britt, developing various new and more expensive "brands" for the local market, followed afterward by the more nimble co-ops. Returning the compliment and closing the circle of mutual admiration expressed by imitation, in 2017 Starbucks announced the opening of a "model farm" tourist destination on the slopes of the Poás Volcano, another icon and tourist destination, a clear recognition of the ingenious success of Café Britt in combining gourmet coffee with ecological tourism.[13]

As the export market was being transformed, the co-ops and their members participated in the most sincere form of flattery, imitation, but with delays of up to a decade. Their attempts to catch up to their rivals and enjoy the high prices for gourmet coffees have had some successes, although certainly more failures. But these efforts took place in a complex context, with sharply falling national harvests (reduced by one-third to one-half in the past quarter century) and increased dedication to the cultivation of "strictly hard"—that is, highest quality—beans, which have doubled as a percentage of the harvest since 2000, all framed within the new "quality competitions" that reward with truly extraordinary prices the production of winning private farms. The co-ops and private processors also paid limited rewards for quality from the 1960s to the 1980s, but these bonuses were essentially based on zones and altitudes in supply areas rather than being awarded to individual farms, and they certainly did not amount to up to ten or twenty times the average purchase price, which is what the modern competitions may offer.

The co-ops face certain limitations when competing in the gourmet market. Their first attempt to compete, after the collapse of the ICA in 1989, ended in failure when the Coffee Co-op Federation (Federación de Cooperativas de Caficultores, or FedeCoop) acquired a roasting facility in Florida. The venture ended in a spectacular bankruptcy and major losses for the eleven coffee co-ops that had invested in the project between 1998 and 2000.[14] During those same years, the Santa Rosa co-op and its subsidiary, San Juanillo, producers of lesser-quality coffee than its sister and neighboring co-op, La Libertad, went broke and disappeared in the midst of the era of depressed prices that followed the collapse of the last ICA.

While it is true that Starbucks and its competitors pay much more for high-quality coffee—estimated by them, for example, at 75% over the base price in the New York commodity markets—by law the co-ops cannot sell more than 11% of their product to a single purchaser, for fear of buyer bankruptcies or extreme dependency. Thus, the strategy the co-ops have followed has been to combine sales to several foreign gourmet firms with the development of direct sales of their own premier brands of roasted coffee, whether whole bean or ground. The struggle in favor of so-called denomination of origin, or patent-like control over the use of geographic names like Tarrazú, symbolizing coffee's quality, has proceeded for several years without definitive results. Our informant, Roque Mata, has led that struggle among the Tarrazú coffee growers.[15]

The messages and images employed by the co-ops have privileged discourses about quality, yes, but above all they emphasize ecology and the direct human relations of small scale. In part owing to the lack of clarity or standards in their international administration, the "green" or "fair trade" labels are not always visible, but the underlying message is. These gourmet co-op brands readily identify their ecological or green strategies, such as by touting a carbon neutral status along with the little frog symbol of the Rainforest Alliance. And just in case it might be necessary, they include the label "café gourmet."

The annual competitions for the designation as the best coffee of Costa Rica have been the most visible novelty within gourmet marketing. Every year, the same regions compete for the crown: Naranjo de Alajuela, Tarrazú, and Dota in the south, sites of renowned co-ops that were strong supporters of the fatal project to roast their coffee in Florida in the late 1990s. The winner of the 2017 competition received more than $8,000 per *fanega* or hundredweight, compared to a base price in New York of less than $140. The speed with which this phenomenon has taken off—and possibly the unreality and unsustainability of these prices—can be appreciated by the fact that the price for the winner in 2016 was slightly less than $6,000, in 2015 it was a little more than $4,000, and in 2014 it was just above $3,000.[16]

Given its novelty—and the prices received to date—one cannot predict the future impact of such competitions, but it clearly not only incentivizes different cultivation practices and scales of processing but also radically disincentivizes traditional forms of organization, within or outside of the co ops. The new firms that compete in this arena combine in novel form different facets of the production process. This refers not only to the so-called *microbeneficios,* processing and roasting coffee in situ, but also to those with their own lands, planted with different coffee varietals that are destined for foreign buyers with whom the growers have contracted beforehand. They work with a variety of types of bushes, not just Caturra, from full-growing, traditional varietals left behind in the Caturra era (Bourbon, Geisha, and others) to recent imports from Kenya and other African and Asian countries. The finance and marketing requirements, in addition to agronomic and processing know-how, are so substantial that the ideal formula for such a firm would be a financier, a broker, and an agronomist, brought together in one or more individuals. If the possible rewards are enormous, so too are the risks, since the initial investment for a *microbeneficio* firm of this kind reaches several hundred thousand dollars, with the assumption of future contracts with individuals and foreign markets as demanding as they are wealthy.[17]

The impact of coffee production's reorganization in the gourmet era is only beginning to define itself. In contrast to the co-op era, when the success of reform elevated practically an entire social class en masse, converting a rural petty bourgeoisie into a much more solvent middling one, the new model increasingly rewards the relatively few who possess direct or close ties to the new, expanded, neoliberal bourgeois classes, specialists in finance, marketing, agronomy, and genetics. This not only reduces the generalized social impact of the transformations of the decades from the 1960s to the 1980s, owing to the radical decrease in the proportion of the national population involved, but also reinforces the same tendencies toward urbanization and professionalization that marked both the success and the sunset of the co-op era.

Costa Rica's success in placing itself in the international gourmet market has also had unexpected consequences, a topic we will explore more thoroughly in chapter 5. As the national harvest has diminished—and no matter how much more dynamic the national roasters become in the proliferation of "quality brands" for domestic consumption—Costa Rica has had to import lower-price and lower-quality coffees to cover domestic demand. By 2016, estimates are that those imports reached some 3,500 tons.[18] Voices are beginning to call for the introduction of the *robusta* varietal (prohibited by law in 1988) in lower altitude areas inhospitable to *arábigo,* to alleviate the shortage.[19]

The proliferation of gourmet brands in the domestic market and the concentration of these smaller harvests in higher-quality beans means that many local consumers have also benefited from a better product. Actually, during periods of low international prices, the domestic market has functioned as an important cushion for growers, since local prices are rather high. But there can be no doubt that the poor cannot pay such high prices and suffer from an obviously lower quality in the coffee they are offered, despite the fact that Costa Ricans continue to consume enormous quantities of coffee, similar to the United States (4.6 kilograms per capita per year), well above Colombia, and exceeded in Latin America only by Brazil (6.1 kilos).[20] Although the words "gentrification" and "yuppification" have not been freely translated to the Costa Rican context, some of their regressive social impacts seem universal. In chapter 5, we will turn our attention to other equally universal facets of the modernization process, both agricultural and societal.

5

Costa Rica After Coffee

Transformations and Unexpected Consequences

The co-op movement arose among Costa Rican coffee growers as a response to what they called a "felt need" to survive, but also to prosper, by receiving a larger share of the international price for their finished product relative to local private processors and merchants. Immediately thereafter, the need arose to participate in the diffusion of a radical improvement in their cultivation practices and productivity, thanks to dwarf variety bushes. However, the success of their productive and organizational strategies was part of a much broader socioeconomic context of profound and rapid transformations, some strengthened and even led by the growers, and others parallel to but disconnected from their sociopolitical positions. In either case, growers had to respond to such transformative processes, inserting themselves into the processes or resisting them, depending on the case, but rarely with a clear understanding of how they were interconnected. This situation sometimes led to what I refer to as unexpected consequences.

Between the mid-twentieth and early twenty-first centuries, Costa Rican society was transformed ever more rapidly, from one in which about half of labor was employed in agriculture to one in which barely 15% is, with similar numbers in terms of gross domestic product. No matter the weight of the coffee co-ops, they could not avoid the withdrawal of finance by the state banks—their firmest ally between 1960 and 1980—from agriculture in general and coffee in particular, to the point of near total disappearance of finance, in the case of coffee, after the crises of the next two decades. Financial backing had been fundamental to the doubling of the national harvest at its high point, but it also showed an inverse tendency to decline following the price crises of the 1990s and the triumph of gourmet coffee's logic of higher quality over greater quantity.[1]

In chapter 3, we shared several emblematic metaphors or jokes from this complex and contradictory experience of the founding generation of the co-ops. Here, we intend to explore in greater detail the global context of these social, economic, and demographic transformations. In each metaphor, one catches a glimpse of a transformation process with enormous implications both for Costa Rican society as a whole and for coffee-growing co-op members in particular. After all, the golden years of coffee cooperativism cleared the way for a Costa Rica after coffee, where coffee and its reduced number of aging growers mattered ever less in national life.

This unexpected transition, far from being a sign of failure, was the product of cooperativism's triumphs, most often thanks to decisions made and paths chosen by growers themselves. Adapting to new situations, the product of the social and economic ascent achieved by their generation, the co-op members' children and grandchildren inherited a world radically transformed in demography, education, land tenure, work, and ecology. The political position of *liberacionismo,* which from the start had been both social democratic and anticommunist, turned ever more conservative and less reformist. However, in the long run, most relevant was the irremediable loss of the political weight of coffee and the co-ops in a Costa Rica ever more urban and less agrarian, with less numerous and better-educated families, now within a population that, when graphed, appears more like a bottle than a pyramid (graphs 3 and 4).

Demographic Transition and New Social Patterns

The most relevant transformation for the historical trajectory and context of coffee cooperativism and for social actors in the course of their lifetimes was undoubtedly the least directly comprehensible in all its profundity. This was a demographic transition, both in its purely vital or population aspects (fertility, mortality, age pyramids, or migration) and in its causes and consequences, such as the revolution taking place in education levels and new gender and marriage patterns. As noted in chapter 3, several of our co-op informants commented on this, joking about "elder excursions" and the "few faces under fifty" or universally lamenting the lack of a replacement generation, owing to the professionalization of children, with their novel university degrees and urban or technical jobs.

The co-op era in Costa Rican history began at the very moment of the

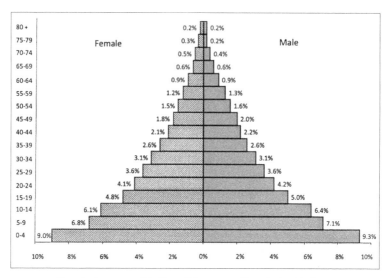

GRAPH 3. Population pyramid: Costa Rica, 1960. (Population Reference Bureau; www.prb.org)

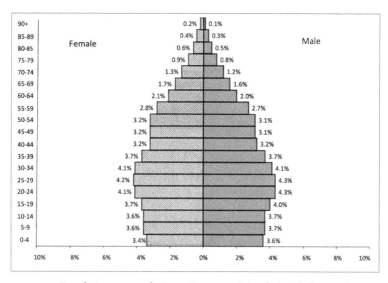

GRAPH 4. Population pyramid: Costa Rica, 2017. (Population Reference Bureau; www.prb.org)

highest rate of population growth and the largest proportion of youthful groups within it. It triumphed, but today the co-ops survive within the framework of a radically aged population and with characteristics and behaviors practically unknown at the time of their founding. Ironically, its triumph contributed enormously to the rise and consolidation of all these changes:

- Radical decline in the native-born population's growth rate, owing to an equally radical reduction in fertility, deep alterations in new household formation patterns, and an ever-increasing postponement of marriage, especially among women with newfound access to higher education and formal economy jobs.
- Simultaneous increases in wealth and inequalities during the neoliberal-era transformation of social class structures, both rural and urban. Among the multiple expressions of this, the most visible has been massive undocumented labor in-migration, which is not only replacing domestic out-migration from the rural areas to the Greater Metropolitan Area (Gran Área Metropolitana) or to the United States but also is in part counteracting, with more numerous children, the national tendency toward stagnation or even decline in the rate of population replacement.
- Aging of co-op coffee growers and new difficulties in finding replacements among the next generations, within the long-term pattern of progressive concentration of coffee growing and a preference toward men in land distribution through inheritance.
- Generalized urbanization of the Central Valley and the displacement of coffee cultivation toward the periphery in general and the far south in particular.

From Children and Adolescents to the Elderly; from Early Marriage to Generalized Postponement

Between 1950 and 1970, Costa Rica achieved unheard-of population growth rates, with nearly half (44.7%) of the population being under fifteen years of age and only 4.8% being older than sixty in 1960 (graph 3). The health, education, and pension systems were built, in large part, to respond to the challenges of that era. Today, with 13.7% of the population over age sixty, there are other pressing challenges, above all those related to the growth of the elderly population and the cost of public sector pensions. In 1960, the challenges included maternal and infant care in public health services, or the building of schools and the training of an ever-increasing number of teachers to fill them, but today only 21.6% of the population is younger than fifteen (graph 4). Between 2001 and 2013, the frequency of households with at least one elderly person went from 25% to 33% and the portion of households with an elderly person living alone went from 12% to nearly 16%. By 2030, it is projected, there will be eighty-seven elderly for each one hundred youths under age fifteen. Life expectancy for the Costa Rican population, which was only sixty-seven in 1970, reached an average of eighty in 2016 (77.5 for men and 82.6 for women).[2]

In general terms, since the mid-twentieth century and the apogee of the demographic boom, each generation of Costa Rican women has given birth to half the number of children that their mothers did, thanks to the extraordinary reduction in mortality, particularly infant mortality. The fertility rate declined from 4.9 in 1970 to 1.9 in 2014. If it were not for the differential behavior of immigrant women (who are younger and more prone to earlier family formation), the native-born population would be characterized by decline, which is typical of practically all developed and postindustrial societies. However, it has been estimated that during the past fifteen years, 12% of children born in Costa Rica have been born to Nicaraguan mothers.

The underlying causes of this demographic change have been the postponement of marriage (as well as an increase in the number of people remaining permanently single) and contraceptive use. Such changes are powerfully associated with urbanization and with greater educational achievement and labor market participation for women in recent times. These processes are typical of late industrial modernization and postmodernity worldwide. But Costa Rica was never industrial, and the delay of marriage, women's high school and university education, their professionalization, and their occupational diversification were historically first associated with one of the populations most impacted by coffee cooperativism, the petty and middling rural bourgeoisie.

The depth of this transformation should not be underestimated. The average age at first marriage or common-law union has increased spectacularly, but so have the frequency of cohabitation without formalizing any union and the number of households headed by women, with these last two cases increasingly involving higher socioeconomic sectors. Just as in northern postindustrial societies, the increase in age at marriage has been notable in Costa Rica in recent times, as has the divergence of urban and rural areas. The age of marriage went from 23 to 25 for men and 19 to 22 for women in the mid-twentieth century, and then to 28.0 and 24.5 in 1992, and to 33.5 and 28.2 in 2012.[3] While it is true that similar increases have occurred in both the United States and Nicaragua (the two most relevant points of comparison as sites of migration), the speed of change has been even greater in Costa Rica than in the United States, and the differences with Nicaragua are also great—at least some two to five years, on average, for younger Nicaraguan spouses.

Other indicators of the profound changes in the character of contemporary marriages abound. The proportion of couples in common-law or informal unions rather than formal marriages went from 17% in 1984 to 33% in 2011. Reflecting greater middle- and upper-class participation in the reconfiguration of marriage, even greater change was noted in the most prosperous and professional districts, the sites of the two largest public universities—San Pedro de Montes de Oca, in San José, and the city center of Heredia. There, the frequency of informal unions was nearly double the national figures, increasing from 6% to 6.5% of unions in 1984 to 24% to 25% in 2011. Even more revealing was the fact that, in 2015, some 3.5% of all households made up of reproductive-age couples were childless, and in 60% of these households, both members worked outside the home. Likewise, the figures on the increase in divorce are crudely revealing. They went from only 10% of marriages in 1980 to 15% in 1990 and 45% in 2016.[4]

All of these figures point not only to the reduction of fertility and the rate of population growth, which leap into view, but also to a rapid and profound redefinition of family formation patterns and women's role therein. As in other regions, as the process of population redistribution toward the Greater Metropolitan Area proceeded, with its feminine predominance and precocious onset of fertility reduction, ever larger regional differences appear in age of marriage, in fertility, and in natural population decline, as well as in household composition.

While it is true that the number of women living in cities, and the percentage of female-headed households, increased with urbanization, as did the frequency of female-headed households living in poverty, it is also true that the proportion of female-headed households with children increased among the middle and upper classes.[5] Thus, we are witnessing generalized phenomena, but with differential impacts for different segments of the population. From 1987 to 2013, the proportion of female-headed households more than doubled, from 17% to 36% (the figures for urban areas were 21% to 40%, and for rural areas 13% to 29%), together with a population resident therein, from 15% to 33%, but those heads of household also radically improved their educational preparation and labor market participation. Owing to rapid urbanization, the number of households living in urban areas went from 46% in 1987 to 63% in 2013, with 70% of female-headed households residing in urban areas by 2013. Though 23% of these heads of household declared themselves to be married or in an informal union in 2013, more than three-quarters headed households without a spouse and declared themselves divorced, separated, widowed, or single.[6]

The educational level of female household heads improved substantially, but at a slower pace than for the female population in general. From 1987 to 2013, the percentage of women fifteen or older who had attended high school grew from 21.1% to 37.4%, and the number with university studies increased even more dramatically, from 7.9% to 20.6%. For heads of household, the figures are from 16% to 32% for secondary school and from 7.6% to 20.2% for university studies. The proportion of heads of household without any formal educational certification was reduced from 13.7% to 5.8%, with the average number of years of study growing from 5.4 years in 1987 to 8.3 years in 2013.

Economic participation in the wage labor market was below 20% for all working-age women in the 1970s; it rose to 32% in 1990, 38% in 2000, and 45% in 2013. Women heads of household entered the labor market at an even higher rate. In 1987, 45% of them participated in the labor market, rising to 58% in 2007 before falling to 54% in 2013, owing to the economic crisis. If one considers completion of high school to be the minimum requirement to compete for wage employment, then women heads of household have long surpassed male heads of household. In 1987, 25% of female and 21% of male heads of household had graduated high school, and in 2013 the figures were 43% for females and 34% for males.

In fact, the most spectacular advances in educational levels have occurred in access to university. In the 1960s, the only public options that existed were the Universidad de Costa Rica or the Teacher's College (Escuela Normal) in Heredia, which became the Universidad Nacional in 1973. These two, along with the Technological Institute (Instituto Tecnológico de Costa Rica) in Cartago, made up the totality of higher education in the country, all three publicly financed. The private universities only began to appear at the end of the 1970s, though with a rapid proliferation and surprising saturation. By 2014 there were sixty-three different institutions—five public, fifty-three private, and five international.[7]

The growth of university enrollments and coverage of the youthful population has been notable. Between 1973 and 2011, the population old enough to have finished university studies (eighteen to twenty-four) increased 3.7 times, but the number of university graduates was multiplied 14.3 times. There were 208,612 students enrolled in higher education in 2014, or 34.2% of the population ages eighteen to twenty-four. Before 1990, at least 80% of the university degrees were conferred by public universities. Through the mid-1990s, the larger proportion of degrees continued to be awarded by public universities, but the numbers turned increasingly in favor of the private universities. In 1995, 43.8% of degrees came from the privates, and 68.5% in 2013. Around half of those who enter a university, whether public or private, are able to earn a degree.

Women's participation in this process has been even more impressive. Between 2000 and 2010, the growth in the number of women university graduates (206.3%) was more than double the figure for men (97.5%). As in the developed world and the most advanced Latin American nations, women represent the clear majority of university graduates in Costa Rica—63.7% in the period 2008 to 2010. Roughly, then, the social transformations have revolved around a profound alteration in women's status, which inevitably implies enormous changes for men as well. Beyond family formation and vital rates, such changes range from the economic sphere to interpersonal, emotional, and domestic relations and are more a reflection than a cause of the underlying process.

Neoliberal Inequalities and the New Normal:
Unemployment, Those Who Study and Work, Those
Who Do Neither, and the Undocumented

While the defenders of the new order praise its real and undeniable achievements, indicators of growing inequality and its negative effect also abound, including a marked social and economic exclusion of certain groups. Similar to the way in which inferior coffees are imported for the domestic market while superior beans are exported (described in chapter 4), the "new normal" distributes opportunities and wealth in radically unequal form. Likewise, the rapid advance of educational attainment and the professionalization of employment entails two other, related phenomena: a persistently high level of unemployment and an enormous number of youth who neither study nor work (the so-called *ninis*) in an economy that, it seems, requires neither their labor nor that of anyone with a lower level of academic preparation than the rising national average.

For more than a decade, the official unemployment rate has remained around 10% or more, regardless of economic expansion or contraction. Although unemployment particularly affects less-educated populations and residents of agricultural zones that lag behind, it also can be explained by the so-called lost generation of the first neoliberal decade (basically, the 1980s), when so many were forced to abandon their studies to contribute to family incomes as unskilled adolescent workers. In effect, that generation never regained their lost years of study, nor did they achieve a better skill level in the labor market, even after the public education system managed to recover from its losses and broaden its coverage from the end of the twentieth century on.

When they abandoned the classroom, the lost generation also witnessed the decay of the earlier system of bureaucratic state employment for high school graduates, and they recognized that their future lay in the new contractual services sector, with jobs or subcontracting in fields from catering and private security to construction, call centers, or the transport industry. During the same era, their older siblings, cousins, and friends very often suffered so-called labor mobility programs, which forced them out of precisely such state bureaucratic positions, and they lost no time trying to finish high school in pursuit of positions disappearing before their eyes.[8] As new economic sectors expanded—in tourism, computing, and services, with their indispensable requirements of foreign languages and technical skills—their labor demand would hardly include these groups. At the same time, undocumented immigrants tended to dominate traditionally unskilled activities such as domestic service, construction, and agriculture, making a bad situation worse.

The associative and solidarity-based solutions privileged between 1940 and 1980, based on institutionalization and incorporation into the formal economy, have increasingly proved incapable of addressing the challenges of this new normal, and informal employment grows nonstop. According to the most pessimistic calculations, informal employment represented 43% of all employment in 2017, while the fiscal costs of creating a new formal sector job continue to rise, presently exceeding 26% of base salary in mandatory benefits and payroll deductions, the highest level in Latin America. According to slightly less pessimistic official figures, of the approximately 2,060,000 persons employed, some 615,175 have positions so precarious they do not contribute to health or pension systems, more than 130,000 are underemployed, and almost 345,000 work more than forty hours per week without earning the minimum salary, clear evidence of the informality of their employment. At the same time, the number of unemployed is estimated at a little more than 200,000 and the monthly income of those who are self-employed is only 260,516 *colones.*[9]

Given the rapid aging of the general population, and contrary to actual reality, the number and amount of contributions to social security would necessarily have to increase in order to avoid the collapse of the pension system, especially of the public sector, which was inherited from the earlier social democratic era. Ironically, another historical reform that ends up contributing to the growth of informal employment is the high minimum wage level, which for decades has been a dead letter in large areas of the national economy, such as agriculture and construction.

Despite exploding university enrollments, there is another face of adolescent experience, a more somber perspective on the labor market and professional aspirations. In the new century, having university studies came to replace high school as the requirement for climbing the first step on the ladder to a middle-class, professional career, giving rise to a new and worrisome phenomenon: the *ninis,* or youth between fifteen and twenty-four years old who neither study nor work. Recent research estimates that around 150,000 Costa Ricans, 17% of the population between those ages, report neither work nor study activities.[10] This is not so much due to dropping out of school, though that is much more frequent in rural than in urban areas, but rather is a form of disguised unemployment or underemployment, affecting all social classes. For comfortable, bourgeois families, it can be a more or less elegant form of social coexistence, hiding the problem and the "at home" shame of children or grandchildren who "fail to launch" and do not become independent until a decade later than was the norm in earlier decades. In fact, it is also related to the radical postponement of marriage among these groups.[11]

Among the more working classes, the phenomenon of the *ninis* is combined with the *"sisis,"* that is, youth who both work and study at the same time—nearly 12% of the population between fifteen and twenty-four years of age.[12] Although in a way they represent the polar opposite of the *ninis* in terms of indicators of initiative and aspiration, these legitimate heirs of the problematic situation of the earlier lost generation of the 1980s are also negatively affected by their limited personal resources and opportunities for advancement at the right time. Together, the *ninis* and the *sisis* comprise at least 30% of youth, and given such situations of relative risk, it is no surprise that social anxiety afflicts more and more of them and their family members.

No matter how much the two coasts and rural areas are statistically identified with the worst indicators in this area, their social, political, and media visibility is concentrated in marginal urban sites and neighborhoods, where physical proximity and opportunities only accentuate and highlight underlying inequalities and the exclusionary dynamic. Urban *ninis* include both those who struggle daily in the informal economy but prefer not to declare any status to surveyors and those who participate in various activities, from irregular to delinquent, to survive or build a future. The impressive proliferation of violent crime and hit men offer eloquent proof of the explosive growth of drug and human trafficking and money laundering, activities that generate their own forms of self-regulation in the shadows, settling scores with extrajudicial killings. The murder rate per 100,000 inhabitants in Costa Rica is still relatively low compared to its northern neighbors, but it has more than doubled since the mid-1990s, from barely five to nearly twelve in 2016.[13] If the national authorities seize around two tons of cocaine per month, one can only imagine the quantities that are successfully trafficked, as well as the number of people (youth especially) involved in or affected by such activities.

The Undocumented at Home and Abroad: Opportunity and Competition

If *tarrazuceños* recall with irony the renaming of wild "coyotes" as "human traffickers" to the United States, they have a harder time comprehending the undocumented among them—their new temporary or permanent neighbors, Nicaraguans and indigenous Ngöbes from the border regions with Panama—as their own equivalents in the neoliberal and postmodern labor supply chain. As the coffee zone most prone to emigration to the United States, New Jersey in particular, during the 1990s, Tarrazú has lived like few others the drama of new systems of agricultural labor and the virtual collapse of earlier labor guarantees, which were based not in union organization but in state intervention, beginning in the 1940s, in favor of citizenship rights, minimum wages, and universal health coverage.

The replacement pattern is even reflected in the numbers reported. Of the just over 125,000 Costa Ricans officially resident in the United States according to the 2010 census, approximately 80,000 were born in Costa Rica. Nearly 20,000 lived in New Jersey—only Los Angeles and Florida reported more. Those who study the undocumented phenomenon estimate the actual total at perhaps double the number officially registered, which implies that thousands of *tarrazuceños* were in the United States by the 1980s, with or without documents. In their place, from 10,000 to 15,000 Ngöbes emigrate each year for the coffee harvest in southern Costa Rica.[14] However, the oldest and most urbanized coffee zones of the Central Valley have also witnessed the complete transformation of the harvest, from family labor recruitment among neighbors to work gangs of outsiders, undocumented or not, without local roots.

This "perfect storm" first gained steam during the late 1980s and dramatically accelerated during the 1990s, the apogee of the Washington Consensus, which was followed by triumphant neoliberalism practically worldwide. Migratory flows, from Nicaragua to Costa Rica and from Costa Rica to the United States, combined winds of expulsion and attraction, push and pull factors, nearly perfectly. Those who fled Nicaragua had the push factor (or headwind) of first the Contra war and then the Sandinista economic collapse, followed by the opposition triumph in 1990, with its renewed faith in the private sector as the solution for Nicaragua's deep problems of employment and poverty. As a pull factor (or tailwind), there first was the expanded Costa Rican labor demand, driven by tropical agriculture on the coasts (both traditional, with bananas, and new, with the rapid growth of pineapple and other crops), which followed the defeat and dismantling of the banana workers union and its historical guide, the Communist Party (whether called *Vanguardia Popular* or another name later on), by the mid-1980s. Almost immediately, Nicaraguan immigrant labor came to dominate in the fields of domestic service, security, and construction, thanks above all to the spectacular growth of the Greater Metropolitan Area (and within it, the new phenomenon of condominiums) and of the beach hotels on the Pacific coast, following the tourism boom of the 1990s. From fewer than 400,000 tourists per year in the mid-1980s, tourism increased to more than 1 million ten years later, and then to more than 2.5 million in 2015, representing about 12% of the national economy and the same percentage of employment.[15]

In Costa Rica, the expulsion and attraction dynamics were equally combined, but in a somewhat different context. After a decade of structural adjustments and growing poverty in the 1980s, the collapse of the ICA in 1989 and the fall of coffee prices in the 1990s, and the resulting rearticulation of the world coffee market, many small coffee growers and farmers with more children than hectares of land available for inheritance said good-bye as those children left for New Jersey or another U.S. destination. For these emigrants, the best option would be to work in the service industry or construction in the North (which experienced its own boom in the decade and a half from the mid-1990s to the beginning of the Great Recession in 2008), rather than competing at home with the local undocumented for wages several times lower and in rapid decline. This was particularly true if their goal was to not just survive but to save, to maintain their landed status or their hope to achieve it in a future return to their native land. Likewise, the emergence of new markets and circuits, especially on the U.S. East Coast—starting with pineapple, continuing on a smaller scale with other fruits and vegetables, and culminating with the present-day massive trafficking of cocaine along the Costa Rican Pacific coast—opened a multitude of new opportunities for agents, employees, and merchants to try their luck in North America rather than confronting labor transformations that did not favor them in Costa Rica in the 1990s.

Studies, surveys, and vox populi all have shown the impact of immigrant labor and noncompliance with minimum wage laws in large sectors of the national economy. When informal employment constitutes nearly half of total employment, it cannot be surprising that many estimate that one-third to one-half of all workers receive incomes below the legal minimums. The sectors most characterized by this phenomenon are, no doubt, agriculture, personal services, and construction. On the other hand, those who defend the rights of the undocumented, of "guest" workers with limited work permits, or of both, as is nearly always the case, have very strik-ing evidence of their contributions to the national economy.

Victor Umaña, the director of the Latin American Center for Com-petitive and Sustainable Development of the Central American Business Administration Institute, claims that 8.5% of the national population is foreign-born, with very diverse labor market participation, comprising 25% of domestic servants, 14% of all agricultural workers (and 50% of sea-sonal workers), 65% of laborers (and 40% of foremen in construction), 4% of bus drivers, and 6% of men who work in security. Likewise, he cal-culates that 12% of gross domestic product is generated with immigrant labor, whose salaries amount to 4.4% of GDP. Where immigrant labor's contribution is most concentrated is in the construction industry, where it represents 4% of GDP and 6% of total national employment. Referring only to Nicaraguan immigrants, he estimates that a quarter of their more than $1 billion in salaries earned in 2014 went as remittances to their home country, and the rest was spent or invested in Costa Rica.[16]

In the coffee sector in particular, the transformation to temporary har-vest labor without local roots is practically universal. Nonetheless, given that this harvest is measured and paid for by amounts collected, not by hours or days worked, minimum salaries have perhaps suffered less dete-rioration than in other agricultural activities. Where deteriorating condi-tions have been most notable has been in two situations: first, in the hir-ing of favored groups (relatives or neighbors) for the first pass through the groves, which is much better paid in hourly terms, and then employ-ing outsiders for the second and third pass through, when there are fewer beans to pick; and second, in the precarious and unhealthy housing condi-tions for harvesters coming from long distances, such as Nicaraguans and Ngöbes whose home villages are far from the Central Valley.[17]

All of my informants commented on this abrupt and jarring transition from the 1980s to the early twenty-first century. Even the largest grow-ers, such as Gerardo Chacón, recalled with a certain nostalgia the time when all of the sixty or seventy harvesters his father hired were from the neighborhood and received their payment in copper coins minted by the owner himself. Guido Rojas recalled with the same nostalgia times when neighbors, both men and women, participated in the harvest, even claim-ing that a certain Danielillo, godson of the then president of the republic,

Daniel Oduber, did so as well.[18] Others recalled how some of them, sons not yet independent of their landed elders, had managed to insert themselves into that small-scale and geographically complex harvest transportation system, buying a pickup in the early 1960s to haul the golden beans or to distribute milk in the neighborhood, after having initially gotten behind the wheel as truck drivers for Tournon or for their own relatives.[19]

Very few of today's outsider harvesters would employ their income to insert themselves into the local coffee production chain in such a way, although the equivalent of the milk route in small retail merchandising has never lost its attraction for the fortunate who manage to leave migration behind and settle permanently in the area.[20] In fact, given the logic of remittances within the prevailing neoliberal model, the transformative impact of the new transnational proletariat's savings are felt more strongly very far from the site of the work being done. This is as true in Costa Rica as it is in the United States.

Inheritance, Gender, Generational Replacement

The challenges of landed inheritance were inserted into profound, parallel processes of sociodemographic and socioeconomic transition. The first half of the twentieth century witnessed a dual process of social polarization (downward social mobility and rapid out-migration among still large families) and the consolidation of a general pattern of land distribution that favored sons. Such a pattern was anything but rigid, and we even encounter women as owners of large coffee farms in the 1955 agricultural census and as members of the co-op in 1971. However, thanks to this restriction and unofficial favoritism, the size of coffee farms could remain stable even before the radical reduction in family size and the abandonment of agriculture by the post-1970s generations.

The challenges of succession soon gave way to other challenges for these more recent generations, with the rapid aging of farmers (and co-op members) combined with the equally rapid urbanization of the majority of Heredia's best coffee lands. They no longer worried about which siblings to exclude from inheriting landed property but about how to recruit at least one farmer. The shrinking number of heirs now occupied non–coffee professional levels of society and were in fact ready to seek greater profits by selling building lots rather than cultivating the family lands. At the same time, the co-ops had to face the consequences of ever-smaller harvests coming from their urbanized surroundings, expanding their purchasing radius to fully occupy their processing plants.

To analyze inheritance patterns in my earlier study, I had only the data for Santo Domingo and its hamlets. Subsequently, the original forms of the 1927 census for San Isidro were discovered, and I repeated my analysis for that district, with practically the same findings. After identifying all siblings in households registered in 1927 in which at least one was among the landowners in the 1955 census, we see the same overrepresentation of sons. Of 27 families registered in San Isidro in 1927, only 8 of 37 members enumerated as owners in 1955 were women, and of 33 families in Santo Domingo, only 9 of 51 were women. Likewise, in Santo Domingo, 46% of 91 males appeared as property owners in 1955, while only 9% of 97 females did, and in San Isidro, 34% of 86 males appeared as property owners but only 13% of 60 females did (table 12). In an area of strong out-migration like San Isidro, this is an indication of a pattern of male preference in land inheritance.

The descriptions offered by my informants show how they themselves interpreted the logic of the succession process they experienced at mid-century. Marco Tulio Zamora Alvarado recalled that all seven siblings could choose between receiving a coffee plot of one *manzana*, along with an experienced field hand assigned to its care (not exactly congruent with his idea of belonging to the group of "paupers"), or its equivalent in cash (20,000 *colones*). Orlando Barquero began his work in coffee taking care

Table 12. Property Ownership among Siblings in 1955

Siblings listed in the 1927 Census	Appeared	Missing	Total Persons	Total Families
Santo Domingo				
Males	42	49	91	
Females	9	88	97	
Total	51	137	188	33
San Isidro				
Males	29	57	86	
Females	8	52	60	
Total	37	109	146	27

Sources: 1927 population and 1955 agricultural censuses.

of a two-*manzana* plot originally destined for his sister's inheritance. He mentioned that all eight siblings were at one time members of the co-op, suggesting that all participated in some way in the family distribution of coffee lands. Similarly, Carlos Villalobos Chacón began managing coffee plots for a great aunt and then combined all sorts of activities and occupations to begin acquiring plots in his own name while traveling his milk route at daybreak.[21]

Gerardo Chacón Chacón had a somewhat different experience, as an heir with his brothers of a larger coffee enterprise. In the 1925 probate of his grandfather, José Chacón Villalobos, his father, José María Chacón Chacón, is listed, along with his six siblings, all brothers. Among them we find four farmers, an artisan, a pharmacist, and a physician. Even though the fortune could not compare with that of the Zamora Chacóns and their Hacienda Zamora, as the most well-off direct relatives of any of our informants, it gave signs as clear as they were precocious of the urban professionalization that would come to characterize the rest. In fact, the first indications of postponement of marriage, as well as occupational migration to the free professions and commerce, appeared among these wealthier farmers in Santo Domingo and San Isidro well before their generalization after the 1970s.[22]

As in nearly all transitions to modern agriculture, whether mechanized or not, the number of surviving farmers is radically reduced as they age. Today, the co-op founding generation faces once again the problem of landed inheritance, this time not as young entrepreneurs but as owners, nearly always of much reduced enterprises. Not only has the position of individuals changed radically, but so has the overall context. Without exception, all of them comment on and lament the lack of a replacement generation—sons or daughters, nephews or nieces, even grandchildren— with sufficient know-how and interest in maintaining the family's coffee tradition. Once again, Gerardo Chacón Chacón is the most extreme case. Even though he has reduced his coffee operations by more than half, as a grower without children he sees no solution. Not even his nephews or nieces seem to have either the interest or the relevant know-how.

Our informants were as insistent as they were eloquent when referring to their own experience of such changes. From Anita Azofeifa, with her enormous efforts as a young widow to educate her ten children with her savings and through novel university scholarships, to Carlos Villalobos, with all his children out of agriculture and placed in offices and ministries, to Guido Rojas, with an agronomist daughter not interested in coffee, to Román Rodríguez, with his only son managing an Internet café—all highlighted an extraordinary upward social and educational mobility in a single generation, even as they lamented the dilemma of coffee groves and inheritance. All had moved ahead with the process of reducing or even practically eliminating their coffee operations, and no one glimpsed a very clear route toward agricultural succession. Rather, all tended toward selling, at least in part, buildable lots as the solution or next step.

Even those children who had pursued careers in agronomy tended to seek employment in other growing export activities, such as pineapple. It was much more common to find them in nonagricultural professional careers linked to even more lucrative technological fields, from medicine and health services (including a medical tourism industry) to call centers for all manner of consulting firms. However counterintuitive such an abrupt occupational transition may seem, public sector recruiters promoting the economic development of the northern Midwest in the United States regularly sell the attractions of its states based on the advanced educational levels of the labor force, as if corn and pigs, wheat and cattle, were no more than a naturalized "environmental effect." The new society of Costa Rica after coffee suffers no greater effects of elision, self-delusion, or selective memory.

Replacement or Disappearance: The Cement and Farmland War

National authorities of the coffee sector have long recognized that coffee is moving rapidly to other areas, above all to the far south and the older peripheries of the Central Valley. As we saw in chapter 4, the transfer of production to the far south has been notable, with the co-ops of that region taking the place previously occupied by those of the Central Valley. The expression "Cement defeats land" was used by Ronald Peters, manager of the Instituto del Café de Costa Rica, when he pointed to the acceleration of the process, particularly due to the growth of the Greater Metropolitan Area, which has converted traditional coffee areas into new suburbs. ICAFE estimates that within the Central Valley, more than 20% of coffee groves have been lost to urban use, and in fact this is the area that shows the least dynamism in the renewal of aged coffee groves, in a country where 40% of groves were planted more than twenty years ago. The industry faces a new transition process, toward smaller but higher-quality harvests. In the past quarter century, the national harvest has declined by nearly half, from 3.5 million *fanegas* in the 1990s to only 1.89 million in 2016–2017, and productivity per hectare has dropped from 31.9 *fanegas* in 2000–2001 to 24.6 in 2015. In this contraction, the proportion of the harvest corresponding to the highest quality ("strictly hard bean") has doubled during the same period, reflecting what has been characterized as coffee's "seeking the mountains" (*buscando montaña*). However, climate change plays a role as powerful as it is unpredictable, with the transfer of planting not only to higher altitudes but also to microclimates suitable for the equally novel *microbeneficios* of the gourmet era. Part of the recent decline in productivity per hectare is owing not only to the lack of in situ renewal of groves but also to the negative effect of global warming, which causes coffee to seek the mountains and the growers to accompany it.[23]

The Central Valley and its coffee growers are the inevitable losers in this historical process, simply due to changing land use and the pressure of a growing population living there. But the lack of a replacement generation is felt more urgently there, in part because greater access to a university education is concentrated there, along with the nonagricultural employment opportunities such education provides. When our Heredia informants expressed the greatest pessimism about the future of coffee cultivation on their lands, they referenced two dilemmas at once: the lack of a replacement generation, on the one hand, and the feverish sale of urbanizable land—the victory of cement over land—on the other. Guidos Rojas and Marco Tulio Zamora, residents of Barrio Socorro, the lands closest to the capital of San José, recognized that their location made their farms much more valuable for urbanization than for agriculture. In a somewhat ironic tone of self-criticism, Zamora revealed that he, too, had sold plots for a "few millions" during the price crises of the 1990s, as a survival strategy, despite being the most committed to the goal of multigenerational succession.

For those who embraced the option of selling to urbanize, another problem gets worse every day. With the proliferation of new gated communities with restricted access and condominiums throughout Heredia's coffee zones, some municipal authorities began to delay or create obstacles to the process by denying water connection permits for new residential projects. Citing unsustainable pressures on the aquifers, these authorities appealed to the Supreme Court, which recently ruled in their favor, at least for lands at higher altitudes in the province of Heredia.[24]

This belated obstacle to the forward march of cement did not stop the process, but it did generate disgust among landowners, including many of our informants. Justifiably, some argued that if the end of the process—universal urbanization—was a given, all that was left to resolve was how, when, and favoring whom? It would be easy, then, to understand the disappointment of landowners like Orlando Barquero. The municipality had given a water connection permit to his gigantic neighbor, the four- or five-star Hotel Bougainvillea (figure 20), right across the street from his home where we had our conversation, while denying it to much smaller condominium projects simply because they had requested it later.

Once again, contradictory images arise from historical experience. The gates of the Hacienda Zamora in the 1950s blocked not only passage but also the historical aspirations of the soon-to-be co-op members. For those now veteran elders, the new "gates," the so-called scissors limiting access to gated communities with private security, were emblematic of both the solution—sales of lots—and a new obstacle in the path—access to water connections for new construction. Marco Tulio Zamora told us about the

FIGURE 20. Hotel Bougainvillea. (Photo from the Hotel Bougainvillea website)

gates of yesteryear, owned by his relatives and the Hacienda Zamora; years later, he coincidentally participated directly in an international political and media event that reveals a great deal about the processes analyzed in this study, as well as the disagreements of historical memory in Costa Rican society after coffee.

Marco Tulio still retained coffee plots that he continued harvesting. One recent afternoon he had to gather around his children and grand-children—his potential replacements—for an uncommon visitor. On the afternoon in question, in June of 2013, Marco Tulio welcomed to his home the Chinese president, Xi Jinping, who had asked his government hosts for a meeting with "a typical Costa Rican family" as part of his brief and busy official visit (figure 21). Offering proof of their deep confusion over what was historically "traditional" and the co-op transformations of coffee's world, the *liberacionista* presidential administration's authorities selected this farmer, seventy-five years old at the time, whose house was barely three or four kilometers from the capitol.

Zamora said he was impressed with the Chinese leader's interest in coffee cultivation and his statement that he, too, had grown up among very hardworking rural cultivators. The rural experiences to which the Chinese

FIGURE 21. Chinese president Xi Jinping's visit to the Zamora Alvarado home in 2013. (Photo from ChinaDaily.com)

president referred were due not only to the accident of birth but also to his father's forced labor sentence as a high official jailed during the Cultural Revolution. In his improvised, live interview on television, Zamora played the selective strings of historical memory with equal grace, emphasizing that his was a third-generation coffee farm, without mentioning how, thanks to the efforts of his own generation in forming co-ops, his life as a coffee grower had been very different from that of his ancestors. Nor did he express his generation's generalized fear for the continuity of coffee cultivation, or how the multigenerational character of the farm might well end with him.[25]

Nonetheless, his neighbors, the "rich" Zamoras, the gatekeepers of yesteryear, did not suffer so over the replacement question and were more receptive to the alternative of selling to urbanize. And it turns out that only they had enough land to be useful for demanding, "scale" buyers. In 2003, much of what had once been the Hacienda Zamora was acquired for the new campus of Colegio Lincoln. Its modern and ample facilities, inaugurated in 2007, occupy some seven hectares.

In one of his commentaries, as shrewd as it was mordant, Marco Tulio explained that another enormous, chain-link-fenced lot, visible from his house, had been cleared of coffee in expectation of an imminent, similar sale "to one of those universities," a purchase that had never closed. The university in question undoubtedly obtained another piece of land for its campus, as one of the fifty-three private institutions created in less than forty years, during and after the golden age of coffee cooperativism and its profound transformations.

Epilogue

The co-op and green and white era of the second half of the last century was characterized by a barely visible turbulence in the placid waters of 1948's triumphant anticommunist reformism. Our informants and their co-op brethren harvested enormous victories and advances, both material and sociopolitical, but they also were aware of the turbulence surrounding them. How could they fail to see it, having gone from peripheral if frequently invoked to central figures in national political life, only to then see their power and influence dissipate, all in a single generation.

They managed not only to consolidate themselves but also to prosper as landowners, even as the reformism they supported nationally opened up endless new, primarily nonagricultural opportunities. Beyond its anticommunism, it was a petty bourgeois reformism, and from that angle, popular, a development model that both social democrats and many socialists of the era supported under the formula of a popular national capitalism. The triumph of this petty bourgeois reformism depended very directly on the local class structure, on the ingenuity and resources of the most solid rural middle-class groups, who managed to double the national coffee harvest precisely during a period of high prices and co-op predominance. The seeds of reform were planted in very fertile lands in the Costa Rican Central Valley in the 1960s and 1970s.

The politics of a green revolution as antidote to red seems to have closed the circle of the anticommunist crusade inspired by the victory in 1948, with the recent rightist turn of a National Liberation Party that no longer offers more than rhetoric in favor of its historic social democratic ideology. Given the profile of today's Costa Rica, more typical of the first world than the third in terms of its native-born population, which is as aged as it is highly educated, the current model privileges a favorable insertion into the world market of commodity production, the creation of free-trade and tax-free zones, as well as subcontracting and other activities involving highly trained labor, leaving social reform ideologies as a distant memory. Competition, not cooperation, is the tonic of the new era, exploiting comparative advantage rather than solidarity.

For the classic theorists of capitalist development, beyond the often dominant and strident anticommunist ideologues, the very idea of a green revolution as antidote to red assumed a broader goal of bourgeois social transformation, one that certainly required agricultural modernization but was never limited to it. As such a transformation proceeded, the impulse in favor of land reform would inevitably dissipate, together with the relevance of those same rural agendas, as the proportion of the population employed in agriculture declined.

The Costa Rican equivalent of a green revolution had its transformative effects from the 1970s to the 1990s, thanks to the dwarf variety bushes. This was much later than the apogee of liberal modernization theories internationally, during the 1950s, with their emphasis on rapid urbanization and a classic, labor-intensive industrialization using labor freed up from agriculture. It also was later than the apogee of *liberacionista* social democratic and statist policies from the 1950s to the 1970s. With ever greater momentum after the mid-1980s, globalized labor flows and reductions in social safety nets meant, ironically, that the golden age of *liberacionista* social democratic ideology and public institution building had come to an end before the full impact of the revolution implied by the switch to Caturra, and its transformation of an emergent and triumphal petty bourgeois in a rapidly depopulated countryside in the Central Valley, was realized. Whether opportunistic or obligated, the PLN's recent rightist turn, far from simply being a reencounter with its anticommunist origins, was possible thanks to those same successes of social and economic transformation achieved by its reformist model.

Those who today complain of the PLN's change of position are all too similar to those who criticized both *calderonismo* and the communists for not having remained faithful to their banana worker base, following its historical debacle and virtual collapse during the 1980s. They confuse fidelity to certain messages, eras, and leaderships with the needs created on the ground by the evolution of social class structures and struggles. Both reformisms had their moments to lead social transformations with important legacies, but both shattered against changing political-historical forces and processes and had to adapt to them.

The most emotive homage to the achievements of the green and white era, one that I have heard in a thousand forms, claims that they transformed the country from one in which every poor child born was a future farm laborer to one in which they represented a future professional. Beyond the hyperbole, there is some truth in the claim, above all in light of explosive university enrollments. However, they not only multiplied the number of professionals in the country but also radically reduced the weight of the coffee sector, the size and predominance of traditional families, and the rural proportion of the population. In Costa Rica after coffee, the new professionals also suffer from unemployment and growing precariousness in this tropical postmodernity. All in all, any cross they bear weighs a bit less than the hunger and illness of yesterday's farm laborers, even when taking into account the twenty additional years they will carry it, thanks to the increase in life expectancy during the same period.

The challenge of our times, and not only in Costa Rica, is to reinvent a reform model to confront the new challenges of growing polarization and inequality. Armed with the examples of ingenuity, tenacity, and perseverance that are given such eloquent voice by our informants, we should not expect less of ourselves. However, far from repeating the experiences and aspirations of that generation, it falls to us to decipher a new form of freedom that leads us not to solidarity but to the even more difficult task of overcoming our new and strange form of coexistence—interconnected as never before, but still, even so, alone together. As Marco Tulio Zamora unforgettably expressed it, the indispensable motivation for the founding of the coffee co-ops in his day was a "felt need." What the felt need will be for the new historical actors of the future as they discover their own route to reform is anything but clear today. What is clear is that they will discover it in a Costa Rica after coffee.

Notes

1. Green Revolution as Antidote to Red in the Green and White Era of National Liberation: Costa Rica's Coffee Co-ops and Anticommunist Reform

1. The original edition appeared in English from Louisiana State University Press in 1986, followed in Spanish from Editorial Costa Rica (ECR) in 1990. It was reissued with a new preface by Editorial de la Universidad Estatal a Distancia (EUNED) in 2009.

2. Jacobo Shifter Sikora, *La fase oculta de la guerra civil de 1948* (San José: EDUCA, 1970); Chester Zelaya Goodman, ed., *Democracia en Costa Rica? Cinco opiniones polémicas* (San José: EUNED, 1977); Lowell Gudmundson, "Costa Rica and 1948: Rethinking the Social Democratic Paradigm," *Latin American Research Review* 19, no. 1 (1984): 35–42. As a first-time professor at the Universidad Nacional in 1975–1976, the first topic that I explored was a reinterpretation of 1940s *calderonismo* as a populist phenomenon. Conversations with Schifter Sikora, then a colleague in the Instituto de Estudios Latinoamericanos, revealed that he had beaten me to the topic. Recent studies have deepened our understanding of *calderonismo* in that era and later, as well as the impact of repression and *liberacionista* hegemony on its memory. See David Díaz Arias, *Crisis social y memorias en lucha: guerra civil en Costa Rica, 1940–1948* (San José: Editorial de la Universidad de Costa Rica [EUCR], 2015); Iván Molina Jiménez, *Los pasados de la memoria: El origen de la Reforma Social en Costa Rica (1938–1943)* (Heredia: EUNA, 2008); Manuel Solís, *Costa Rica: reformismo socialdemócrata o liberal?* (San José: FLACSO, 1992); and Solis, *La institucionalidad ajena: Los años cuarenta y el fin de siglo* (San José: EUCR, 2006).

3. Lowell Gudmundson, "Peasant, Farmer, Proletarian: Class Formation in a Smallholder Coffee Economy, 1850–1950," *Hispanic American Historical Review* 69, no. 2 (1989): 221–57; published in Spanish as "Campesino, granjero, proletario: Formación de clase en una economía cafetalera de pequeños propietarios, 1850–1950," in *Café, sociedad y relaciones de poder en América Latina*, ed. Mario Samper K., William Roseberry, and Lowell Gudmundson (Heredia: EUNA, 2001), 183–242. See also "On Paths Not Taken: Merchant Capital and Coffee Production in Costa Rica's Central Valley," in *The Global Coffee Economy in Africa, Asia, and Latin America*, ed. Steven Topik and William Gervase Clarence-Smith (Cambridge: Cambridge University Press, 2003), 335–59; published in Spanish as "Sobre las vías no elegidas: capital comercial y producción cafetalera en el Valle Central de Costa Rica," *Revista de Historia* 46: 149–84.

4. Lowell Gudmundson, "On Green Revolutions and Golden Beans: Memories and Met-

aphors of Costa Rican Coffee Co-op Founders," *Agricultural History* 88, no. 4 (Fall 2014): 538–65. I refer here to the interviews with the founders of the Polish Jewish community in the book I coauthored with Jacobo Schifter and Mario Solera, *El judío en Costa Rica* (San José: EUNED, 1979).

5. Samuel Huntington, *The Clash of Civilizations and the Remaking of World Order* (New York: Simon & Schuster, 1998), is perhaps the most noteworthy of the many books of the time that sought to find new bases for the defense industries, imperialism abroad, and political ethnocentrism at home, whether it was called "white nationalism" or not. These topics drew the attention of the news media in the late 1990s as the initial triumphal "end of history" style began to fade in the face of post–Cold War realities. For a sharp critique of the multiple and contradictory connections between Huntington's ideas and the Trump phenomenon, see Carlos Lozada, "Samuel Huntington: A Prophet for the Trump Era," *Washington Post* (July 18, 2017).

6. Sherry Turkle, *Alone Together: Why We Expect More from Technology and Less from Each Other* (New York: Basic Books, 2011).

7. The biography industry surrounding William Jennings Bryan continues to generate titles, dozens to this point. Iván Molina Jiménez employs a Costa Rican case with the same theme of the anti-Darwinian struggle against "monkeys" to explore modernity and its local critics; see Jiménez, *La ciudad de los monos: Roberto Brenes Mesen, los católicos heredianos y el conflicto cultural de 1907 en Costa Rica,* 2nd ed. (San José: Heredia: EUNA, 2002). With abundant reasons, many have seen populist aspects, traditions, and styles in the democratic administrations of President Franklin Roosevelt (1933–1945). Their versions of "Janus-faced" populism come into sharp focus in the peculiar coalition of ultraconservative Southern segregationists and social democratic Northern labor unionists in favor the New Deal of the 1930s. That coalition survived for several decades during and after World War II, without resolving its internal contradictions, before crumbling after president Lyndon Johnson supported the dismantling of racial segregation in the 1960s. Johnson's support handed the Southern white and ultraconservative vote to Republicans willing to follow the "Southern strategy," developed first by Richard Nixon in the elections of 1968 and 1972 and faithfully followed thereafter, from Ronald Reagan in 1980 to Donald Trump in 2016.

8. For much broader, recent comparative analyses, see John Abromelt et al., eds., *Transformations of Populism in Europe and the Americas: History and Recent Tendencies* (London: Bloomsbury Academic, 2017). For a collection that analyzes only very contemporary Latin American expressions of left-populism, see Carlos de la Torre and Cynthia Arnson, eds., *Latin American Populism in the Twenty-First Century* (Baltimore: Johns Hopkins University Press, 2013). Another very ambitious comparative project was recently convened by Italian social scientists, to better understand the global phenomenon today, no doubt inspired much more by their own experience with Silvio Berlusconi than with Benito Mussolini. The classic Latin American studies are Michael Conniff, *Latin American Populism in Comparative Perspective* (Albuquerque: University of New Mexico Press, 1981); and Conniff, ed., *Populism in Latin America* (Tuscaloosa: University of Alabama Press, 1999), the second edition of which appeared 2012.

9. A comparative analysis that helps to explain reform and reaction trajectories, based on the type of labor prevalent in the major export activity and the nationality of its proprietors/owners, can be found in Charles Bergquist, *Labor in Latin America: Comparative Es-*

says on Chile, Argentina, Venezuela, and Colombia (Stanford, CA: Stanford University Press, 1986). In the cultural history field, there is an abundance of metaphorical literary classics that employ regions, population, crops, or races to represent supposedly national essences. No doubt the most famous is Fernando Ortiz, *Contrapunteo cubano del tabaco y el azúcar* (Habana: Jesús Montero Editor, 1940). Carlos Luís Fallas, *Mamita Yunai*, which has appeared in several editions since 1940, carried out, to a certain point, the same task in Costa Rica.

10. Rafael Piñeiro, Mathew Rhodes-Purdy, and Fernando Rosenblatt, "The Engagement Curve: Populism and Political Engagement in Latin America," *Latin American Research Review* 51, no. 4 (2016): 3–23.

11. See Constantino Urcuyo, "Diez tesis sobre el populismo," *La Nación* (December 18, 2016); a video interview appeared in the digital version of the same newspaper on March 13, 2017. Other intellectuals who have joined the chorus warning of the local danger of a reborn populism include the editorialists Juan Carlos Hidalgo, "Amenaza populista," *La Nación* (June 4, 2017), and Alfonso J. Álvarez Rojas, "El nuevo populismo," *La Nación* (June 3, 2017).

12. The classic study by Richard Hofstader, *The Paranoid Style in American Politics* (reprint; New York: Vintage, 2008), was done by a Jewish author observing the virulently anticommunist populism of the McCarthy era in the midst of the Cold War. The current proliferation of "fake news" via social media is only the latest version of politics based on conspiracy theories and feverish imaginations, to which left-liberalism is not immune. Perhaps the word it shares the most with the right is "corrupt(ion)." Its use as an epithet, tirelessly these days, as if it were synonymous with all imaginable evils, calls my attention not only as a citizen but as a university professor. It almost sounds like a catechist's admonition: "All the saved, those in favor of human rights and environmental protection, over here; the rest, the corrupt, over there."

13. Ernesto Laclau, *Política e ideología en la teoría marxista: Capitalismo, fascismo, populismo* (Madrid: Siglo XXI, 2015 (originally published in English by New Left Books, 1977); and Laclau, *La razón populista* (México: Fondo de Cultura Económica, 2006 (published in English as *On Populist Reason* by Verso, 2007).

14. Díaz Arias, *Crisis social,* 207–8, 282.

15. Charles Ameringer, *Don Pepe: A Political Biography of José Figueres of Costa Rica* (Albuquerque: University of New Mexico Press, 1979), 31; cited in Julie Charlip, "Pretending to Be Peaceful: Costa Rica's Public Forces, 1940s–1980s" (CLAH Annual Meetings, New Orleans, January 3–6, 2013), 2. If history repeats itself first as tragedy and then as farce, what better example than the braggadocio of José Figueres Ferrer's son, José María Figueres Olsen, also a *liberacionista* ex-president, who unlike the other two former presidents accused of corruption chose not to return to the country to face charges against him. As recently as 2017, in the final televised debate among *liberacionista* candidates seeking the presidential nomination, with his best *machista* and populist pose, Figueres Olsen claimed that he was the only one of the three men on the stage with "the balls" to make difficult decisions. His playing the "Trump card" did not produce the desired results for his failed campaign, but others seeking to represent parties and smaller groups lined up to try their own luck in the time of populism's rebirth.

16. Juan Bosch, *Apuntes para una interpretación de la historia costarricense* (San José: Eloy Morúa Carrillo, 1963).

17. Iván Molina Jiménez, *Anticomunismo reformista* (San José: ECR, 2016).

18. Diane E. Davis, *Discipline and Development: Middle Classes and Prosperity in East Asia and Latin America* (Cambridge: Cambridge University Press, 2004). In his brief essay, Garin Burbank long ago observed equally conservative tendencies inherent to reformist success by American and Canadian agricultural cooperatives. See Burbank, "Agrarian Socialism in Saskatchewan and Oklahoma: Short-Run Radicalism, Long-Run Conservatism," *Agricultural History* 51 (1977): 173–80.

19. Aviva Chomsky, "West Indian Workers in Costa Rican Radical and Nationalist Ideology, 1900–1950," *The Americas* 51, no. 1 (1994), 11–40. See also the documentary edited collections of the most prolific and famous Costa Rican anti-imperialists, Vicente Sáenz and Carlos Luis Fallas, in Mario Oliva Medina and Gilberto López, eds., *Colección Vicente Sáenz,* 6 volumes (San José: Editoriales Universitarias Públicas Costarricenses, 2013); and Carlos Luis Fallas, *De mi vida,* vols. 1 and 2 (Heredia: EUNA, 2013).

20. Rodrigo Facio, *Estudio sobre economía costarricense* (San José: Editorial Zurco, 1942); Carlos Monge Alfaro, *Historia de Costa Rica* (San José: Editorial Fondo de la Cultura, 1947). For an analysis of the use of these ideas by Rodrigo Facio and José Figueres during the 1940s, see Mauricio Menjívar Ochoa, "Contienda política y uso del pasado en la Costa Rica de los años 40: La retórica de Rodrigo Facio y de José Figueres Ferrer, 1939–1951," in *Historia y Memoria: Perspectivas teóricas y metodológicas, Cuadernos de Ciencias Sociales* 135 (San José: FLACSO, 2005). Another example of these debates, their ideological complexities, and the confusion of partisan positions can be seen in the polemic regarding the interpretation of the degree of concentrated ownership of land cultivated with coffee. On the one hand are Carolyn Hall, *El café y el desarrollo histórico-geográfico de Costa Rica* (San José: ECR, 1976); and Yolanda Baires Martínez, "Las transacciones inmobiliarias en el Valle Central y la expansión cafetalera de Costa Rica (1800–1850)," *Avances de Investigación* 1 (San José: Universidad de Costa Rica, 1978). On the other hand is the Brazilian geographer Moretzsohn de Andrade, "Decadencia do campesinato costariqueno," *Revista Geográfica* (Río de Janeiro) 66 (1967): 136–52. Even more definitive data is provided in Carolyn Hall, *Costa Rica: A Geographical Interpretation in Historical Perspective* (Boulder, CO: Westview Press, 1985). For the communist vote in Santo Domingo, see Iván Molina, "El desempeño electoral del Partido Comunista de Costa Rica (1931–1948)," *Revista Parlamentaria* (Costa Rica) 7, no. 1 (April 1999): 491–521.

21. Carmen Kordick, "Tarrazú: Coffee, Migration, and Nation Building in Rural Costa Rica, 1824–2008" (PhD diss., Yale University, 2012) suggests that anger over state actions leading to the 1948 conflict had to do primarily with the hatred of the Treasury police *(Resguardo)* and their violent attempts to suppress illegal alcohol production in the region.

22. *La Nación* (April 12, 2017).

23. Interview with Rafael Naranjo Barrantes at his home in San Marcos de Tarrazú, March 6, 2009.

2. Informants and Their Ancestors in Heredia: The Founding Generation in the Census and Probate Records

1. Gudmundson, "Campesino, granjero, proletario."

2. See Gudmundson, "On Green Revolutions and Golden Beans." Thanks to all my in-

formants for their patience and collaboration, to my colleague Wilson Picado for sharing data from his ongoing research, as well as to Mauricio Meléndez for his genealogical data for Santo Domingo, based in part on the study by German Bolaños Zamora, "Familias fundadoras de Santo Domingo de Heredia" (unpublished manuscript).

3. The classic study of Costa Rican coffee culture was, no doubt, Hall, *El café*, but for our purposes the greatest detail on the family-farm basis of production at the height of the co-op expansion can be found in Ciska Raventós, "Desarrollo económico y contradicciones sociales en la producción del café," *Revista de Historia* 14 (1986): 179–195, which is based on census data from the 1980–1981 harvest; and José Cazanga, *Las cooperativas de caficultores en Costa Rica* (San José: EUCR, 1987). In addition to the study by Cazanga, there are two other recent studies of the co-ops in areas of expanding production, in Naranjo (Alajuela), Johnny A. Mora, *La vía cooperativa de desarrollo del agro: El caso de Coopronaranjo R. L.* (Heredia: EUNA, 2007); and to the south, in San Isidro de El General, Deborah Sick, *Farmers of the Golden Bean: Costa Rican Households and the Global Coffee Economy* (Dekalb: Northern Illinois University Press, 1999).

4. The 1971 list can be found in Archivo Nacional de Costa Rica (ANCR), Trabajo y Seguridad Social no. 56, "La Libertad." The various censuses, from 1846, 1927, and 1955, as well as the probate files, are the same ones used in Gudmundson, "Campesino, granjero, proletario," except for the information for San Isidro in 1927, which was discovered and cataloged later. ANCR, Congreso no. 5424 (1846); Estadística y Censos, Censo de Población, 1927, no. 201–205 (Santo Domingo) and 297–299 (San Isidro); Sección Mortuales de Heredia (630 cases from Santo Domingo and San Isidro, 1840–1940); microfilm from the archives of the Dirección General de Estadística y Censos, rolls 83 and 85. Thanks to Wilson Picado Umaña for his data on processing plants, from his coauthored study with Rafael Díaz, "Reubicando la producción cafetalera en las montañas: Calidad, mercado y cambio climático en Costa Rica," ponencia presentada en el Simposio Indicaciones geográficas y desarrollo regional: Experiencias latinoamericanas en el siglo XXI, 55 Congreso Internacional de Americanistas, El Salvador, 12–17 de julio de 2015.

5. For further discussion and examples, see chapter 5 of the present volume.

6. Gudmundson, "Campesino, granjero, proletario," 193.

7. Gudmundson, "Campesino, granjero, proletario," 218–221.

8. Interview with Marco Tulio Zamora Alvarado at his home in Barrio Socorro, Santo Domingo, March 17, 2009.

9. Interview with Gerardo Chacón Chacón at his home in Santo Tomás de Santo Domingo, March 25, 2009.

10. The classic studies of the Rohrmoser and Tournon firms are by Hall, *El café*; and Gertrud Peters Solórzano, "La formación territorial de las grandes fincas de café en la Meseta Central: estudio de la firma Tournon: 1877–1955," *Revista de Historia* 9–10 (1980): 81–167.

11. In addition to Carlos Naranjo Gutiérrez, "Los sistemas de beneficiado del café costarricense: 1830–1914," *Revista de Historia* 55–56 (January–December 2007): 39–71, there are lists of a few processors in Santo Domingo in 1878 (ANCR, Gobernación no. 28957) and 1887 (ANCR, Fomento no. 35). At least three later probate inventories mention processing plants among the properties to be distributed in inheritance. See ANCR, Heredia, Juzgado Contencioso no. 4901 (Manuel Zamora Chacón, 1918); Juzgado Contencioso no. 852 (Ramón

Villalobos Fonseca, 1895, with two plants and a capital worth of 202,469 pesos, double that of any other deceased individual of the era); and Mortuales Independientes de Heredia no. 2769 (Ramón Villalobos González, 1890). The 1935 figures are from *Revista del Instituto de Defensa del Café* 5 (1937): 185, 301.

12. Orlando Barquero retold me Amado Sánchez's joke in an interview in his home in Santo Tomás de Santo Domingo, March 19, 2009.

13. The coffee processing data identified in note 4 lists all the processing plants operating for each harvest year.

14. Orlando Barquero described the succession of processing plant purchases, confirming what other informants had commented on. Many interviewees repeated the critique of the Santa Rosa co-op as a low-altitude, lower-quality coffee producer.

15. Interview with Carlos Villalobos Chacón at his home in Los Ángeles de Santo Domingo, April 23, 2009. The preeminence of the Villaloboses is reflected once again by the fact that, from 1890 to 1920, two of the three individuals whose probate inventories had processing plants were identified with that surname.

16. From notes taken at the district assembly meeting of La Libertad in San Isidro (March 9, 2009) and the general assembly in San Pedro de Barva (April 4, 2009).

17. On the rise of production in formerly peripheral regions, see Mora, *La vía cooperativa*; Sick, *Farmers of the Golden Bean*; Wilson Picado Umaña, "Territorio de coyotes, agroecosistemas y cambio tecnológico en una región cafetalera de Costa Rica," *Revista de Historia* 59–60 (2009), 119–65; and Umaña, "Des-Conexiones de la Revolución Verde: Estado y cambio tecnológico en la agricultura de Costa Rica durante el período 1940 y 1980" (PhD diss., Universidad de Santiago de Compostela, 2012).

18. Interview with Marco Tulio Zamora Alvarado.

19. I have several times employed this descriptive or prototypical form to paint a picture of social groups in the rural world, and its original inspiration comes from the pioneering work by Fernando Picó, *Amargo café: Los pequeños y medianos caficultores de Utuado en la segunda mitad del siglo XIX* (San Juan: Ediciones Huracán, 1981). In addition to the already cited interviews with Marco Tulio Zamora Alvarado, Orlando Barquero Barquero, Gerardo Chacón Chacón, and Carlos Villalobos Chacón, I interviewed Román Rodríguez Argüello at his house in San Francisco de San Isidro, on April 15, 2009.

20. ANCR, Mortuales Independientes de Heredia no. 4596; and the 1927 census for Santo Domingo.

3. Green Revolutions and Golden Beans: The Founding Generation's Memories and Metaphors

1. Gudmundson, "Campesino, granjero, proletario; Gudmundson, "On Paths Not Taken." The coffee literature, with its powerfully structuralist focus and limitations, is reviewed in the edited volume Topik and Clarence-Smith, *Global Coffee Economy*, as well as in Mario Samper K., William Roseberry, and Lowell Gudmundson, eds., *Café, sociedad y relaciones de poder en América Latina* (Heredia: EUNA, 2001).

2. Fabrice Lehoucq and Iván Molina, *Stuffing the Ballot Box: Fraud, Electoral Reform, and Democratization in Costa Rica* (Cambridge: Cambridge University Press, 2002); James Ma-

honey, *The Legacies of Liberalism: Path Dependence and Political Regimes in Central America* (Baltimore: Johns Hopkins University Press, 2001); Jeffery M. Paige, *Coffee and Power: Revolution and the Rise of Democracy in Central America* (Cambridge, MA: Harvard University Press, 1997); Robert Williams, *States and Social Evolution: Coffee and the Rise of National Governments in Central America* (Chapel Hill: University of North Carolina Press, 1994); Deborah J. Yashar, *Demanding Democracy: Reform and Reaction in Costa Rica and Guatemala, 1870s–1950s* (Stanford, CA: Stanford University Press, 1997).

3. Daniel James, *Doña María's Story: Life History, Memory, and Political Identity* (Durham, NC: Duke University Press, 2001) offers a key example of the advantages of a careful reading of informant testimony as labor history. The most notable Central American examples come from Jeffrey Gould, *To Lead As Equals: Rural Protest and Political Consciousness in Chinandega, Nicaragua, 1912–1979* (Chapel Hill: University of North Carolina Press, 1990), which is based on detailed interviews with Nicaraguan peasants displaced by the cotton boom of the 1960s and 1970s, whose struggles converged with the Sandinista insurrection. Gould later coproduced two documentary films on El Salvador focused on the suppression of indigenous identity following the 1932 massacre and the rise of liberation theology in the 1970s, both powerfully dependent on testimonies and oral history interrogated with similar discursive concepts. See Jeffrey Gould and Carlos Henríquez Consalvi, dirs., *1932: Scars of Memory (Cicatriz de la memoria)* (New York: First Run/Icarus Films, 2002); and Gould and Consalvi, *The Word in the Woods (La palabra en el bosque)* (New York: Films Media Group, 2012). Paige, *Coffee and Power* amounts to a discursive analysis of his late 1980s conversations with members of the Costa Rican coffee elite and represents something like the other side of the historical coin, recounted here by former harvest suppliers converted into co-op founders. Kordick, "Tarrazú" includes interviews with several of the same people we spoke with in Tarrazú and gives their testimony a close reading in search of multiple meanings for gender relations, violence, and migration to and from New Jersey.

4. Cazanga, *Las cooperativas* is another key "informant" for this chapter. See also Sick, *Farmers of the Golden Bean;* and Mora, *La vía cooperativa.*

5. James Scott, *Weapons of the Weak: Everyday Forms of Peasant Resistance* (New Haven, CT: Yale University Press, 1987).

6. The classic study of family-size farm productivity at the height of the co-op movement's influence is Raventós, "Desarrollo económico y contradicciones sociales."

7. Interview with Marco Tulio Zamora Alvarado at his home in Barrio Socorro, Santo Domingo, March 17 2009.

8. Interview with José Flores at his home in San Marcos de Tarrazú, March 13, 2009. See also Kordick, "Tarrazú." Picado, "Territorio de coyotes," 134–36, suggests that the terracing innovations alone were responsible for 50% of the improvement of output per hectare in Tarrazú.

9. The material for this and the following two paragraphs comes from an interview with Eduardo Villalón at his home in San Pedro, Montes de Oca, San José, April 3, 2009.

10. Kordick, "Tarrazú," 328.

11. D. Clayton Brown, *Electricity for Rural America: The Fight for the REA* (Westport, CT: Greenwood Press, 1980); David Nye, *Electrifying America: Social Meanings of a New Technology* (Cambridge, MA: MIT Press, 1990), Audra J. Wolfe, "'How Not to Electrocute the

Farmer': Assessing Attitudes Towards Electrification on American Farms, 1920–1940," *Agricultural History* 74, no. 2 (Spring 2000): 515–29.

12. Interview with Noé López at his home in Tarrazú, March 27, 2009. His equivalent in the Banco Nacional in Santo Domingo de Heredia was Óscar Córdoba, uniformly remembered fondly by informants there as a tireless co-op promoter.

13. The firm of the French immigrant family Tournon is the best-studied example among the large-scale processors in all of Costa Rica. Ironically, those responsible for this microscopic attention were themselves identified, by national origin, with the commercial competition. The English historical geographer Carolyn Hall (*El café y el desarrollo*) pioneered this work and also was responsible for the postgraduate training of Gertrud Peters Solórzano, member of a family of major coffee exporters of German descent. See Peters Solórzano, "La formación territorial."

14. Interview with Jorge Villalobos at his home in San Josecito de San Isidro de Heredia, April 23, 2009.

15. Interview with Carlos Villalobos at his home in Los Ángeles de Santo Domingo, April 23, 2009.

16. Interview with Román Rodríguez at his home in San Francisco de Santo Domingo, April 21, 2009.

17. Gertrud Peters and Margarita Torres, "Las disposiciones legales del Gobierno costarricense sobre los bienes de los alemanes durante la Segunda Guerra Mundial," *Anuario de Estudios Centroamericanos* 28, no. 1–2 (2002): 137–159; Gertrud Peters Solórzano, *El negocio del café de Costa Rica, el capital alemán y la geopolítica, 1907–1936* (Heredia: EUNA, 2016). Noé López recalled the first manager of the Tarrazú co-op, Rafael Sauren Witz, who was of German descent and married to a local woman. Numerous examples of individuals and technical influences of German origin are discussed in Mora, *La vía cooperativa*. For broader studies of Germans in Costa Rica during this era, see Christine C. Nemcick, "Germans, Costa Ricans, or a Question of Dual Nationalist Sentiments? The German Community in Costa Rica, 1850–1950" (PhD diss., Indiana University, 2001); and Carlos Albrecht, "A Resilient Elite: German Costa Ricans and the Second World War" (PhD diss., University of York, 2010).

18. Interview with Orlando Barquero at his home in Santo Tomás de Santo Domingo, March 19, 2009.

19. Interview with José Flores.

20. Interview with Román Rodríguez.

21. Interview with Roque Mata Naranjo at his home in Tarrazú, March 27, 2009.

22. Kordick, "Tarrazú" includes interview material with *tarrazuceños* in New Jersey and their family members in Costa Rica as well as much more limited interviews with the new immigrant workers in Tarrazú. See also Patricia Alvarenga, *Trabajadores inmigrantes en la caficultura* (San José: FLACSO, 2000).

23. Interview with Orlando Barquero.

24. Interview with Anita Azofeifa at her home in San Isidro de Heredia, March 26, 2009.

25. In addition to Azofeifa's lament about the aged faces, Guido Rojas also noted the same pattern of their children pursuing technical degrees in non-coffee-related agriculture, during an interview at his home in Barrio Socorro, Santo Domingo, April 20, 2009.

26. Interview with José Cazanga at his office at the Universidad Nacional in Heredia, April 29, 2009; Cazanga, *Las cooperativas de caficultores.*

4. From Co-op Reformism to Gourmet Globalization: Java Joe, Juan Valdez, Starbucks, and Café Britt

1. William Roseberry, "The Rise of Yuppie Coffees and the Reimagination of Class in the United States," *American Anthropologist* 98, no. 4 (1996): 762–75; Michael Jiménez, "De la plantación a la taza de café: Café y capitalismo en los Estados Unidos, 1830–1930," in *Café, sociedad y relaciones de poder en América Latina,* ed. Mario Samper K., William Roseberry, and Lowell Gudmundson (Heredia: EUNA, 2001), 73–110. There are at least two important studies of coffee consumption and quality in Costa Rica: Patricia Vega Jiménez, *Con sabor a tertulia: Historia del consumo del café en Costa Rica (1840–1940)* (San José: EUCR, 2004); and Ronny J. Viales Hurtado and Andrea M. Montero Mora, *La construcción sociohistórica de la calidad del café y del banano de Costa Rica: Un análisis comparado 1890–1950* (San José: UCR Centro de Investigaciones Históricas de América Central, 2010). The best study of the world coffee market during the International Coffee Agreement and how it responded to its collapse is Robert Bates, *Open-Economy Politics: The Political Economy of the World Coffee Trade* (Princeton, NJ: Princeton University Press, 1999).

2. For the history of the co-op in Naranjo, see Mora, *La via cooperativa;* for San Isidro de El General, see Sick, *Farmers of the Golden Bean;* and for Tarrazú and Dota, see *La Nación,* August 15, 2016; Picado Umaña, "Territorio de coyotes"; and Picado Umaña, "Conexiones de la Revolución Verde."

3. The data employed in graphs 1 and 2 provide the basis for calculating percentages of co-op regional production and come from the Ministerio de Agricultura. They were given to me by Wilson Picado from his research in progress. I thank him for this and other gracious assistance.

4. *La Nación,* August 15, 2016.

5. See note 3.

6. Jiménez, "De la plantación a la taza," 38.

7. As if it were a joke in bad taste, the firm that considers itself the producer of the "best" hot dogs, Nathan's Famous, sponsors this competition—another example, even in the midst of the postmodern gourmet era, of how humor and spectacle win out over "quality" messaging in this "top-of-the-line" enterprise. The senselessness of this sort of event was crudely revealed in early 2017 in Denver, Colorado, in one of the local events imitating the Nathan's spectacle, when a participant suddenly died in the middle of the competition.

8. David McCreery, *Rural Guatemala: 1760–1940* (Stanford, CA: Stanford University Press, 1994); McCreery, personal communication.

9. It is revealing to compare the current marketing strategy of Starbucks (and other gourmet coffees) with that of enterprises that still maintain the Fordist formula of yesteryear: lowest common denominator humor. While Starbucks is absent from mass media and its television ads, its competitor in New England, Dunkin' Donuts, employs entertainment and sports celebrities in jocular situations to the point of saturation on television and radio. The firm began in New England, where it has a dominant presence, although it has some 11,000

shops in thirty-six countries. It maintains its foundational legacy as a distributor of doughnuts more than quality coffee, since the very name of the company reminds the consumer that the function of the cup of hot liquid is to wet the doughnut before eating it.

10. There is an extensive literature on Juan Valdez, even a recent thesis written by Fernando Augusto Gracia, "In Search of Juan Valdez: The Juan Valdez Marketing Campaign and the Construction of Colombian Identity" (master's thesis, Bryn Mawr College, 2011).

11. The images described here appeared primarily in the onboard magazine of American Airlines (*American Way*) during the late 1980s and early 1990s.

12. All of the information here about the gourmet market in the 1980s and 1990s comes from Roseberry, "Rise of Yuppie Coffees." We should better define the term "yuppie," which appeared in the press for the first time in 1980 and was broadly diffused later in the United States and the United Kingdom. Its alternative meanings are "young, upwardly mobile professional" or "young urban professional." I prefer the former, once again with the key word for my analysis, "upward," suggesting the imaginative and behavioral class content of bourgeoisification and extreme self-absorption. Thus, it is employed not only as adjective and noun but also in reference to the transformative process of individuals and social sectors with the expression "yuppification." In fact, the word "yuppification" has strong links with another, used later in the 1990s, "gentrification," to refer to the conversion of entire poor urban neighborhood to luxurious residences, precisely for these clearly ascendant young professionals. This term for the reconversion of urban space at the end of the twentieth century is derived from the word "gentry," or rural landed bourgeoisie, used primarily in England. "Yuppie" also represents something of a recycling of the word "hippie," associated with that mid-1960s generation, long-haired, ostentatiously disdainful of consumer society, with a preference for marijuana and rock music, culminating in the Woodstock festival in 1969. "Hippie" itself comes from "hipster," or an admirer of the Beat Generation of poets of the 1950s, above all in San Francisco, epicenter of the hippie phenomenon in the 1960s as well. Curiously, once again in California, "hipster" returned as part of twenty-first-century jargon to refer to the second or third yuppie generation in urban centers.

13. The figures for Starbucks and Café Britt are from their own websites and from Wikipedia. The purchase of the experimental farm by Starbucks and the development of new varietals were reported several times by ICAFE on its website, in the weekly *El Financiero*, by *La Nación,* and in various US media, such as the *Wall Street Journal* and *Seattle Times* (March 18, 2013). The opening of the visitor center was also widely reported (*Tico Times,* March 29, 2017).

14. Mora, *La vía cooperativa,* 217–21.

15. "Café de Los Santos está a un paso de obtener su denominación de origen," *La Nación,* May 3, 2017. On the opening of gourmet coffeehouses in Costa Rica, see *La Nación,* October 18, 2016.

16. *La Nación,* June 21, 2016, and June 28, 2017. First place prizes have continued to spiral, reaching $10,000 in 2019.

17. The recent agrarian experience of Guatemala offers intriguing comparisons, not only with coffee production for niche markets abroad but even more with the massive exports of vegetables (broccoli, peas, and the like), both of which are in indigenous hands. See Edward F. Fischer and Bart Victor, "High-End Coffee and Smallholding Growers in Guate-

mala," *Latin American Research Review* 49, no. 1 (2014): 155–77; Edward F. Fischer and Peter Benson, *Broccoli and Desire: Global Connections and Maya Struggles in Postwar Guatemala* (Stanford, CA: Stanford University Press, 2006). There currently is a research project under way at the Escuela de Historia of the Universidad Nacional, which focuses on *microbeneficios* in Costa Rica.

18. *La Nación,* July 26, 2016.

19. *La Nación,* September 15 and October 10, 2016.

20. *La Nación,* February 16, 2017.

5. *Costa Rica After Coffee: Transformations and Unexpected Consequences*

1. Mora, *La vía cooperativa,* 203–9. For more detail on the process, see Jorge León et al., *Historia económica de Costa Rica en el siglo XX,* tomo 1, *Crecimiento y políticas económicas* (San José: EUCR, 2014). Jarring examples of this process of financial expansion and contraction abound. Far from losing its rhythm with the closing of the Intel factory, for instance, financial backing moved to its major replacement, the medical device sector, which reported exports for the first half of 2017 that nearly equaled the value of all agricultural exports combined during the same period. *La Nacion,* August 17, 2017.

2. The figures for this and the following paragraph come from the Population Reference Bureau of the United Nations, Department of Economic and Social Affairs, Population Division; Gilbert Brenes, "Cambio demográfico y heterogeneidad geográfica, 1978–2008," in *Estado de la Nación: Decimoquinto informe estado de la nación en desarrollo humano sostenible* (San José, 2009); Natalia Díaz Zeledón, "La elección de vivir sin tener hijos," *La Nación,* August 14, 2016; and *La Nación,* October 17, 2016.

3. Instituto Nacional de Estadísticas y Censos de Costa Rica (INEC), *Panorama Demográfico, Año 2012* (vol. 1, Año 7), 17. United Nations, Population Reference Bureau, *World Fertility Report, 2012,* offers the following ages for women in Costa Rica who marry for the first time: 19.1 (1976), 23.8 (1995), and 28.2 (2010). For men, ages are 26.8 in 1995 and 31.7 in 2010. Given that both sources calculate the age at first "marriage," they overstate a bit the postponement of the formation of unions, in view of the doubling or more of the frequency of informal unions during the same period. In the United States between 2010 and 2014, the average age at first marriage for woman varied from 23.8 in Utah to 29.3 in Massachusetts. Similar differences are found between the Greater Metropolitan Area and the most highly rural areas of Costa Rica.

4. *La Nación,* August 14, 2016, according to figures from the Encuesta de Hogares of 2015 by the Instituto Nacional de Estadística y Censos. On divorce, see *La Nación,* February 25, 2017. On informal unions, see the study by the journalist and analyst Hassel Fallas, "Gráfico interactivo: Más parejas conviven sin casarse en Costa Rica," Ladatacuenta Datacounts, February 3, 2017, https://hasselfallas.com/2017/02/03/grafico-interactivo-mas-parejas-conviven-sin-casarse-en-costa-rica.

5. For another analysis of this paradoxical phenomenon of women in poverty and in the professions, and their responses to social change, see Silvia Chant, "La 'femenización de la pobreza' en Costa Rica: un problema para las mujeres y los niños?," *Anuario de Estudios*

Centroamericanos 33–34 (2009), 205–60.

6. The source for this and the following two paragraphs is Natalia Morales Aguilar and Isabel Román Vega, "Principales transformaciones en el perfil de los hogares con jefatura femenina en Costa Rica en los últimos veinticinco años (1987–2013)," in *Vigésimo Informe Estado de la Nación en desarrollo humano sostenible* (San José: Programa del Estado de la Nación, 2013).

7. The source for the expansion of university enrollments and women's participation in them is *Quinto Informe del Estado de la Educación* (San José: Programa del Estado de la Nación, 2015).

8. For a revealing analysis of this reality, see Susan E. Mannon, *City of Flowers: An Ethnography of Social and Economic Change in Costa Rica's Central Valley* (New York: Oxford University Press, 2016).

9. Juan Carlos Hidalgo, "Alto desempleo," *La Nación,* May 21, 2017; Álvaro Trejos, "Realidades económicas, 2014–2017," *La Nación,* June 24, 2017.

10. Abril Gordienko, "Una sola Costa Rica?," *La Nación,* April 28, 2016; Fraser Pirie R., "La generación de los ninis," *La Nación,* May 17, 2017.

11. Mannon, *City of Flowers* offers cases as striking as they are illustrative, in her portrait of Heredia, the City of Flowers, during the neoliberal era.

12. Gordienko, "Una sola Costa Rica?"

13. Michael Krumholtz, "Costa Rica Suffered through Most Violent Year on Record in 2016," *Tico Times,* January 3, 2017.

14. Wilson Garro Mora, "La coyuntura migratoria en el cantón de Tarrazú: representaciones sociales sobre la migración transnacional en el marco de las transformaciones actuales," *Revista Rupturas* 6, no. 2 (July–December 2016). For a broader analysis of both the indigenous immigrants and the *tarrazuceños* returning to the area, see Lenin Mondal López and Gustavo Amador Hernández, *Diagnóstico socioeconómico y de oportunidades de mercado para la población migrante de la subregión de Los Santos* (San José: EUNED, 2014). Even including all the undocumented Costa Ricans in the United States, the figures are still very modest compared to the numbers for its Central American or Mexican neighbors. See also J. Cervantes, *Perfil de la población de origen costarricense en Estados Unidos* (México: Centro de Estudios Monetarios Latinoamericanos: November 2012).

15. The figures on tourism's increase are from Wikipedia (in Spanish).

16. "Impacto económico del migrante," *La Nación,* December 7, 2016.

17. Patricia Alvarenga, *Trabajadores inmigrantes en la caficultura* (San José: FLACSO, 2000). On the topic of Nicaraguans in Costa Rica in general, see Carlos Sandoval García, *Otros amenazantes: Los nicaraguenses y la formacion de identidades nacionales en Costa Rica* (San José: EUCR, 2002).

18. Interviews with Gerardo Chacón and Guido Rojas.

19. Interviews with Marco Tulio Zamora and with Rafael Ulate Barquero, in Santa Rosa de Santo Domingo, March 23, 2009.

20. Randall Zúñiga, "Chiriticos: de la travesía a la pertenencia," *La Nación,* April 17, 2016.

21. Interviews with Zamora, Barquero, and Villalobos.

22. Gudmundson, "Campesino, granjero, proletario," 207–8; ANCR, Mortuales Independientes de Heredia, R 1168, no. 244 (José Chacón Villalobos, 1925). For the heirs of the

Hacienda Zamora, see ANCR, Mortuales Independientes de Heredia, no. 4596; and the 1927 census for Santo Domingo.

23. The data on harvests, yields, and displacements owing to urbanization and climate change come from *La Nación*, October 6, 2016; and March 30 and 31, 2017; *CentralAmerica-Data.com* news, December 14, 2015, and August 31, 2016, citing the statement by Peters; Melissa Allison, "Climate Change Takes Toll on Coffee Growers, Drinkers Too," *Seattle Times*, March 5, 2011; and Picado and Díaz, "Reubicando la producción cafetalera en las montañas."

24. The court's ruling in favor of the suspension of water connection permits for large construction projects in Heredia was reported in *La Nación*, June 18, 2015.

25. *Telenoticias*, June 3, 2013; *La Nación*, June 4, 2013, 6A; *ChinaDaily.com*, June 5, 2013.

Bibliography

Abromelt, John, Gary Marotta, Bridget María Chesterton, and York Norman, eds. *Transformations of Populism in Europe and the Americas: History and Recent Tendencies*. London: Bloomsbury Academic, 2017.

Albrecht, Carlos. "A Resilient Elite: German Costa Ricans and the Second World War." PhD diss., University of York, 2010.

Allison, Melissa. "Climate Change Takes Toll on Coffee Growers, Drinkers Too." *Seattle Times* (March 5, 2011).

Alvarenga Venutolo, Patricia. *Trabajadores inmigrantes en la caficultura*. San José: FLACSO, 2000.

Alvarez Rojas, Alfonso J. "El nuevo populismo." *La Nación* (June 3, 2017).

Ameringer, Charles. *Don Pepe: A Political Biography of Jose Figueres of Costa Rica*. Albuquerque: University of New Mexico Press, 1979.

Baires Martinez, Yolanda. "Las transacciones inmobiliarias en el Valle Central y la expansión cafetalera de Costa Rica (1800–1850)." In *Avances de Investigación*, no. 1. San José: Universidad de Costa Rica, 1978.

Bates, Robert. *Open-Economy Politics: The Political Economy of the World Coffee Trade*. Princeton, NJ: Princeton University Press, 1997.

Bergquist, Charles. *Labor in Latin America: Comparative Essays on Chile, Argentina, Venezuela, and Colombia*. Stanford, CA: Stanford University Press, 1986.

Bolaños Zamora, German. "Familias fundadoras de Santo Domingo de Heredia." Unpublished manuscript.

Bosch, Juan. *Apuntes para una interpretación de la historia costarricense*. San José: Eloy Morúa Carrillo, 1963.

Brenes, Gilbert. "Cambio demográfico y heterogeneidad geográfica, 1978–2008." In *Estado de la Nación: Decimoquinto informe estado de la nación en desarrollo humano sostenible*. San José, 2009.

Brown, D. Clayton. *Electricity for Rural America: The Fight for the REA*. Westport, CT: Greenwood Press, 1980.

Burbank, Garin. "Agrarian Socialism in Saskatchewan and Oklahoma: Short-Run Radicalism, Long-Run Conservatism." *Agricultural History* 51 (1977): 173–80.

Cazanga, José. *Las cooperativas de caficultores en Costa Rica*. San José: EUCR, 1987.

Cervantes, J. *Perfil de la población de origen costarricense en Estados Unidos*. México: Centro de Estudios Monetarios Latinoamericanos, 2012.

Chant, Silvia. "La 'femenización de la pobreza' en Costa Rica: un problema para las mujeres y los niños?." *Anuario de Estudios Centroamericanos* 33–34 (2009): 205–60.

Charlip, Julie. "Pretending to Be Peaceful: Costa Rica's Public Forces, 1940s–1980s." CLAH Annual Meetings, New Orleans, January 3–6, 2013.

Chomsky, Aviva. "West Indian Workers in Costa Rican Radical and Nationalist Ideology, 1900–1950." *The Americas* 51, no. 1 (1994): 11–40.

Conniff, Michael. *Latin American Populism in Comparative Perspective*. Albuquerque: University of New Mexico Press, 1981.

———, ed. *Populism in Latin America*. Tuscaloosa: University of Alabama Press, 1999.

———, ed. *Populism in Latin America*. 2nd ed. Tuscaloosa: University of Alabama Press, 2012.

Davis, Diane E. *Discipline and Development: Middle Classes and Prosperity in East Asia and Latin America*. Cambridge: Cambridge University Press, 2004.

De Andrade, Moretzsohn. "Decadencia do campesinato costariqueno." *Revista Geográfica* (Río de Janeiro) 66 (1967): 136–52.

De la Torre, Carlos, and Cynthia Arnson, eds. *Latin American Populism in the Twenty-First Century*. Baltimore: Johns Hopkins University Press, 2013.

Díaz Arias, David. *Crisis social y memorias en lucha: guerra civil en Costa Rica, 1940–1948*. San Jose: EUCR, 2015.

Díaz Zeledón, Natalia. "La elección de vivir sin tener hijos." *La Nación* (August 14, 2016).

Facio, Rodrigo. *Estudio sobre economía costarricense*. San José: Editorial Zurco, 1942.

Fallas, Carlos Luís. *Mamita Yunai*. San José, 1940.

———. *De mi vida, tomos I y II*. Heredia: EUNA, 2013.

Fallas, Hassel. "Gráfico interactivo: Más parejas conviven sin casarse en Costa Rica." Ladatacuenta Datacounts, February 3, 2017, https://hasselfallas.com/2017/02/03/grafico-interactivo-mas-parejas-conviven-sin-casarse-en-costa-rica.

Fischer, Edward F., and Peter Benson. *Broccoli and Desire: Global Connections and Maya Struggles in Postwar Guatemala*. Stanford, CA: Stanford University Press, 2006.

Fischer, Edward F., and Bart Victor. "High-End Coffee and Smallholding Growers in Guatemala." *Latin American Research Review* 49, no. 1 (2014): 155–77.

Garro Mora, Wilson. "La coyuntura migratoria en el cantón de Tarrazú: representaciones sociales sobre la migración transnacional en el marco de las transformaciones actuales." *Revista Rupturas* 6, no. 2 (July–December 2016).

Gould, Jeffrey. *To Lead as Equals: Rural Protest and Political Consciousness in Chinandega, Nicaragua, 1912–1979*. Chapel Hill: University of North Carolina Press, 1990.

Gould, Jeffrey, and Carlos Henríquez Consalvi, dirs. *1932: Scars of Memory (Cicatriz de la memoria)*. New York: First Run/Icarus Films, 2002.

———. *The Word in the Woods (La palabra en el bosque)*. New York: Films Media Group, 2012.

Gracia, Fernando Augusto. "In Search of Juan Valdez: The Juan Valdez Marketing Campaign and the Construction of Colombian Identity." Master's thesis, Bryn Mawr College, 2011.

Gudmundson, Lowell. "Costa Rica and 1948: Rethinking the Social Democratic Paradigm." *Latin American Research Review* 19, no. 1 (1984): 35–42.

———. "On Green Revolutions and Golden Beans: Memories and Metaphors of Costa Rican Coffee Co-op Founders." *Agricultural History* 88, no. 4 (Fall 2014): 538–65.

———. "On Paths Not Taken: Merchant Capital and Coffee Production in Costa Rica's Central Valley." In *The Global Coffee Economy in Africa, Asia, and Latin America*, ed. Steven Topik and William Gervase Clarence-Smith, 335–59. Cambridge: Cambridge University Press, 2003. Spanish version in *Revista de Historia* 46: 149–84.

———. "Peasant, Farmer, Proletarian: Class Formation in a Smallholder Coffee Economy, 1850–1950." *Hispanic American Historical Review* 69, no. 2 (1989): 221–57. Spanish version: "Campesino, granjero, proletario: Formación de clase en una economía cafetalera de pequeños propietarios, 1850–1950." In *Café, sociedad y relaciones de poder en América Latina*, ed. Mario Samper K., William Roseberry, and Lowell Gudmundson, 183–242. Heredia: EUNA: 2001.

Hall, Carolyn. *El café y el desarrollo histórico-geográfico de Costa Rica*. San José: ECR, 1976.

———. *Costa Rica: A Geographical Interpretation in Historical Perspective*. Boulder, CO: Westview Press, 1985.

Hidalgo, Juan Carlos. "Amenaza populista." *La Nación* (June 4, 2017).

Hofstader, Richard. *The Paranoid Style in American Politics*. New York: Vintage, 2008.

Huntington, Samuel. *The Clash of Civilizations and the Remaking of World Order*. New York: Simon & Schuster, 1998.

Institute Servicio Técnico Inter-Americano de Cooperación Agrícola (STICA) and the Institute of Inter-American Affairs Food Supply Mission to Costa

Rica. *Progress in Agriculture in Costa Rica: Summary Report 1942–1948*. Washington, DC: Food Supply Division, Institution of Inter-American Affairs, 1949.

Instituto Nacional de Estadísticas y Censos de Costa Rica (INEC). *Panorama Demográfico, Año 2012* (vol. 1, Año 7).

James, Daniel. *Doña María's Story: Life History, Memory, and Political Identity*. Durham, NC: Duke University Press, 2001.

Jiménez, Michael. "De la plantación a la taza de café: Café y capitalismo en los Estados Unidos, 1830–1930." In *Café, sociedad y relaciones de poder en America Latina*, ed. Mario Samper K., William Roseberry, and Lowell Gudmundson, 73–110. Heredia: EUNA, 2001.

Kordick, Carmen. *The Saints of Progress: A History of Coffee, Migration, and Costa Rican National Identity*. Tuscaloosa: University of Alabama Press, 2019.

———. "Tarrazú: Coffee, Migration, and Nation Building in Rural Costa Rica, 1824–2008." PhD diss., Yale University, 2012.

Laclau, Ernesto. *Política e ideología en la teoría marxista: Capitalismo, fascismo, populismo*. Madrid: Siglo XXI, 2015. Originally published in English by New Left Books, 1977.

———. *La razón populista*. 2nd ed. México: Fondo de Cultura Económica, 2006. Published in English as *On Populist Reason*. London: Verso, 2007.

Lehoucq, Fabrice e Iván Molina. *Stuffing the Ballot Box: Fraud, Electoral Reform, and Democratization in Costa Rica*. Cambridge: Cambridge University Press, 2002.

León, Jorge, Justo Aguilar, Manuel Chacón, Gertrud Peters, Antonio Jara, and María Lourdes Villalobos. *Historia económica de Costa Rica en el siglo XX*. Tomo 1: *Crecimiento y políticas económicas*. San José: EUCR, 2014.

Lozada, Carlos. "Samuel Huntington: A Prophet for the Trump Era." *Washington Post* (July 23, 2017).

Mahoney, James. *The Legacies of Liberalism: Path Dependence and Political Regimes in Central America*. Baltimore: Johns Hopkins University Press, 2001.

Mannon, Susan E. *City of Flowers: An Ethnography of Social and Economic Change in Costa Rica's Central Valley*. New York: Oxford University Press, 2016.

McCreery, David. *Rural Guatemala, 1760–1940*. Stanford, CA: Stanford University Press, 1994.

Menjívar Ochoa, Mauricio. "Contienda política y uso del pasado en la Costa Rica de los años 40: La retórica de Rodrigo Facio y de José Figueres Ferrer, 1939–1951." In *Historia y Memoria: Perspectivas teóricas y metodológicas, Cuadernos de Ciencias Sociales* 135. San José: FLACSO, 2005.

Merz, Carlos. "Estructura social y económica de la industria del café en Costa

Rica: Estudio estadístico-analítico." *Revista de Instituto para la Defensa del Café* 5, no. 30–38 (1937).

Molina Jiménez, Iván. *Anticomunismo reformista*. San José: ECR, 2016.

———. *La ciudad de los monos: Roberto Brenes Mesen, los católicos heredianos y el conflicto cultural de 1907 en Costa Rica*. 2nd ed. San José: EUNA, 2002.

———. "El desempeño electoral del Partido Comunista de Costa Rica (1931–1948)." *Revista Parlementaria* (Costa Rica) 7, no. 1 (April 1999): 491–521.

———. *Los pasados de la memoria: El origen de la Reforma Social en Costa Rica (1938–1943)*. Heredia: EUNA, 2008.

Mondal López, Lenin, and Gustavo Amador Hernández. *Diagnóstico socioeconómico y de oportunidades de mercado para la población migrante de la subregión de Los Santos*. San José: EUNED, 2014.

Monge Alfaro, Carlos. *Historia de Costa Rica*. San José: Editorial Fondo de la Cultura, 1947.

Mora A., Johnny A. *La vía cooperativa de desarrollo del agro: El caso de Coopronaranjo R.L.* Heredia: EUNA, 2007.

Morales Aguilar, Natalia, and Isabel Román Vega. "Principales transformaciones en el perfil de los hogares con jefatura femenina en Costa Rica en los últimos veinticinco años (1987–2013)." *Vigésimo Informe Estado de la Nación en desarrollo humano sostenible*. San José: Programa del Estado de la Nación, 2013.

Naranjo Gutiérrez, Carlos. "Los sistemas de beneficiado del café costarricense: 1830–1914." *Revista de Historia* 55–56 (January–December 2007): 39–71.

Nemcick, Christine C. "Germans, Costa Ricans, or a Question of Dual Nationalist Sentiments? The German Community in Costa Rica, 1850–1950." PhD diss., Indiana University, 2001.

Nye, David. *Electrifying America: Social Meanings of a New Technology*. Cambridge, MA: MIT Press, 1990.

Oliva Medina, Mario, and Gilberto Lópes, eds. *Colección Vicente Sáenz*. 6 volumes. San José: Editoriales Universitarias Públicas Costarricenses, 2013.

Ortíz, Fernando. *Contrapunteo cubano del tabaco y el azúcar*. Habana: Jesús Montero Editor, 1940.

Paige, Jeffery M. *Coffee and Power: Revolution and the Rise of Democracy in Central America*. Cambridge, MA: Harvard University Press, 1997.

Peters, Gertrud, and Margarita Torres. "Las disposiciones legales del gobierno costarricense sobre los bienes de los alemanes durante la Segunda Guerra Mundial." *Anuario de Estudios Centroamericanos* 28, no. 1–2 (2002): 137–59.

Peters Solórzano, Gertrud. "La formación territorial de las grandes fincas de café en la Meseta Central: estudio de la firma Tournon: 1877–1955." *Revista de Historia* 9–10 (1980): 81–167.

————. *El negocio del café de Costa Rica, el capital alemán y la geopolítica, 1907–1936*. Heredia: EUNA, 2016.

Picado Umaña, Wilson. "Conexiones de la Revolución Verde: Estado y cambio tecnológico en la agricultura de Costa Rica durante el período 1940 y 1980." PhD diss., Universidad de Santiago de Compostela, 2012.

————. "Territorio de coyotes, agroecosistemas y cambio tecnológico en una región cafetalera de Costa Rica." *Revista de Historia* 59–60 (2009): 119–65.

Picado Umaña, Wilson, and Rafael Díaz. "Reubicando la producción cafetalera en las montañas: Calidad, mercado y cambio climático en Costa Rica." Ponencia presentada en el Simposio "Indicaciones geográficas y desarrollo regional: Experiencias latinoamericanas en el siglo XXI," 55 Congreso Internacional de Americanistas, El Salvador, 2015.

Picó, Fernando. *Amargo café: Los pequeños y medianos caficultores de Utuado en la segunda mitad del siglo XIX*. San Juan: Ediciones Huracán, 1981.

Piñeiro, Rafael, Mathew Rhodes-Purdy, and Fernando Rosenblatt. "The Engagement Curve: Populism and Political Engagement in Latin America." *Latin American Research Review* 51, no. 4 (2016): 3–23.

Population Reference Bureau. *World Fertility Report*. New York: United Nations, 2012.

Quinto Informe del Estado de la Educación. San José: Programa del Estado de la Nación, 2015.

Raventós, Ciska. "Desarrollo económico y contradicciones sociales en la producción del café." *Revista de Historia* 14 (1986): 179–95.

Roseberry, William. "The Rise of Yuppie Coffees and the Reimagination of Class in the United States." *American Anthropologist* 98, no. 4 (1996): 762–75.

Samper K., Mario, William Roseberry, and Lowell Gudmundson, eds. *Café, sociedad y relaciones de poder en América Latina*. Heredia: EUNA, 2001.

Sandoval García, Carlos. *Otros amenazantes: Los nicaragüenses y la formación de identidades nacionales en Costa Rica*. San José: EUCR, 2002.

Schifter Sikora, Jacobo. *La fase oculta de la guerra civil de 1948*. San José: EDUCA, 1970.

Schifter Sikora, Jacobo, Lowell Gudmundson, and Mario Solera. *El judío en Costa Rica*. San José: EUNED, 1979.

Scott, James. *Weapons of the Weak: Everyday Forms of Peasant Resistance*. New Haven, CT: Yale University Press, 1987.

Sick, Deborah. *Farmers of the Golden Bean: Costa Rican Households and the Global Coffee Economy*. Dekalb: Northern Illinois University Press, 1999.

Solís, Manuel. *Costa Rica: ¿reformismo socialdemócrata o liberal?*. San José: FLACSO, 1992.

———. *La institucionalidad ajena: Los años cuarenta y el fin de siglo.* San José: EUCR, 2006.

Turkle, Sherry. *Alone Together: Why We Expect More From Technology and Less From Each Other.* New York: Basic Books, 2011.

Urcuyo, Constantino. "Diez tesis sobre el populismo." *La Nación* (December 18, 2016).

———. "Diálogos con Constantino Urcuyo." *La Nación* (March 13, 2017). Video interview. https://www.nacion.com/el-pais/politica/dialogos-con-constantino-urcuyo/73142223-b7fc-4aa0-a8f7-32354c7ef810/video.

Vega Jiménez, Patricia. *Con sabor a tertulia: Historia del consumo del café en Costa Rica (1840–1940).* San José: EUCR, 2004.

Viales Hurtado, Ronny J., and Andrea M. Montero Mora. *La construcción sociohistórica de la calidad del café y del banano de Costa Rica: Un análisis comparado 1890–1950.* San José: UCR Centro de Investigaciones Históricas de América Central, 2010.

Williams, Robert. *States and Social Evolution: Coffee and the Rise of National Governments in Central America.* Chapel Hill: University of North Carolina Press, 1994.

Wolfe, Audra J. "'How Not to Electrocute the Farmer': Assessing Attitudes Towards Electrification on American Farms, 1920–1940." *Agricultural History* 74, no. 2 (Spring 2000): 515–29.

Yashar, Deborah J. *Demanding Democracy: Reform and Reaction in Costa Rica and Guatemala, 1870s–1950s.* Stanford, CA: Stanford University Press, 1997.

Zelaya Goodman, Chester, ed. *Democracia en Costa Rica? Cinco opiniones polémicas.* San José: EUNED, 1977.

Zúñiga, Randall. "Chiriticos: de la travesía a la pertenencia," *La Nación* (April 17, 2016)

Index

Note: page numbers in *italics* refer to illustrations; those followed by "n" indicate endnotes.

CPSIA information can be obtained
at www.ICGtesting.com
Printed in the USA
LVHW111449011021
699239LV00001B/88